# TROUBLE I'VE SEEN

"Drew Hart masterfully cuts through all the platitudes and good intentions to reach the fleshy, beating heart of true justice. An unforgettable read, *Trouble I've Seen* deserves the church's full attention and considered action. It certainly challenged and changed me."

—RACHEL HELD EVANS, BESTSELLING AUTHOR OF *A YEAR OF BIBLICAL WOMANHOOD* AND *SEARCHING FOR SUNDAY*

"In a critical moment of American history, Drew Hart has given us a book that is vital for the church. *Trouble I've Seen* captures the complexity of race in its systemic and personal consequences and points us to why race should be central to any Christian's life as a follower of Jesus. It is a book for people who are just beginning this journey and for those of us who need encouragement along the way."

—BRIAN BANTUM, ASSOCIATE PROFESSOR OF THEOLOGY, SEATTLE PACIFIC UNIVERSITY AND SEMINARY

"Drew Hart offers himself—his life, his story, his tears, his fire—in the most vulnerable way in the hopes of interrupting the vulgar disposability of black lives in our society. This book is a gift from the heart of one of the sharpest young theologians in this country. Hold it carefully, and allow it to transform you—and our blood-stained streets. *Trouble I've Seen* will move you to do something about the ugly residue of racism that still haunts us."

**—SHANE CLAIBORNE, AUTHOR OF *THE IRRESISTIBLE REVOLUTION***

"Drew Hart makes a courageous and compelling call to the church to get on the road to racial reconciliation and righteousness. He provides practical insights and deep theological reflections in this challenging and necessary resource. You won't be comfortable with this read, but you will be led into the deep waters of the social dilemma and reality of the race matrix. In the end, there is an opportunity for the church to be a bridge over these troubled waters."

**—EFREM SMITH, PRESIDENT AND CEO OF WORLD IMPACT AND AUTHOR OF *THE POST-BLACK & POST-WHITE CHURCH***

"*Trouble I've Seen* makes it plain: in repenting of white supremacy, we have nothing to lose and everything to be liberated from. Hart refuses to silence two gospel scandals that cannot be separated: that in Christ, Pharaoh's armies are invited into the Promised Land, but the only way in is through the waters, where 'Pharaoh's supremacy' and his chariots are 'drown-ded.' This is the saving solidarity of Christ's cross."

**—JARROD MCKENNA, AWARD-WINNING PEACE ACTIVIST AND COFOUNDER OF FIRST HOME PROJECT**

"Drew Hart is an emerging voice in the one of the most difficult conversations facing the church today—the reality and ongoing effects of white supremacy in American Christianity. He challenges the church to take a long, hard look at its complicity with the racism that still permeates our society and to be transformed in thought, word, and deed by the gospel of Jesus Christ. A provocative, powerful, and necessary book."

**—JOHN R. FRANKE, THEOLOGIAN IN RESIDENCE, SECOND PRESBYTERIAN CHURCH, INDIANAPOLIS**

# TROUBLE I'VE SEEN

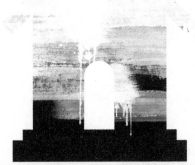

## CHANGING THE WAY
### THE CHURCH VIEWS RACISM
# DREW G. I. HART

**H̵ERALD**
**P R E S S**

Harrisonburg, Virginia

Herald Press
PO Box 866, Harrisonburg, Virginia 22803
www.HeraldPress.com

**Library of Congress Cataloging-in-Publication Data**
Names: Hart, Drew G. I.
Title: Trouble I've seen : changing the way the church views racism / Drew
     G.I. Hart.
Description: Harrisonburg : Herald Press, 2016.
Identifiers: LCCN 2015036574 | ISBN 9781513800004 (pbk. : alk. paper)
Subjects: LCSH: Race relations--Religious aspects--Christianity. |
     Racism--Religious aspects--Christianity.
Classification: LCC BT734.2 .H273 2016 | DDC 277.3/083089--dc23 LC record
available at http://lccn.loc.gov/2015036574

TROUBLE I'VE SEEN
© 2016 by Herald Press, Harrisonburg, Virginia 22802. 800-245-7894.
     All rights reserved.
Library of Congress Control Number: 2015036574
International Standard Book Number: 978-1-5138-0000-4 (paper);
     978-1-5138-0046-2 (hardcover)
Printed in United States of America
Cover and interior design by Reuben Graham

24 23 22 21 20          16 15 14 13 12 11 10 9 8 7

*To Micah and Dietrich*

# CONTENTS

# FOREWORD
## by Christena Cleveland

**R**eader, brace yourself! *Trouble I've Seen*, one of the best books I've encountered on race and Christian faith, will illuminate and challenge the assumptions that you don't even know you possess. It is crucial for Christians to dig deep beneath the surface-level acknowledgments that we make about race and begin to excavate the unspoken ideas and deadly but silent motivations that hover below our conscious awareness.

As individualistic Westerners, many of us haven't considered how our attitudes and behaviors are significantly shaped by our social environment. We think we are independent-minded agents who are unaffected by our environment. But that couldn't be further from the truth. For example, imagine encountering a group of teenagers who have suddenly begun behaving like elderly adults. What would you wonder? What conclusions would you make about these teenagers?

This is the perplexing situation that social psychologist John Bargh faced when he decided to investigate how thoughts, emotions, and behaviors are influenced by unconscious processes—that is, processes that affect us even when we don't know that they are affecting us. In his now-famous study, Bargh asked one group of college students to play a word game involving neutral words, such as *apple*, *sailboat*, and *film*. He asked another group to play a word game involving words that are closely associated with

stereotypes of elderly people, such as *wrinkle, bingo,* and *Florida.*
After each college student completed the word game, he or she
was thanked for participating in the study and then asked to leave.

But Bargh and his research team continued their observation,
measuring how long it took each participant to exit the labora-
tory and walk to the elevator at the end of the hall. Astonishingly,
Bargh discovered that the college students who had played the
word game with the elderly stereotype words *walked more slowly*
than the students who had played with neutral words! Bargh con-
cluded that words like *bingo* activated the elderly stereotype in a
college student's mind, which then prompted the student to walk
more slowly. As a result of simply being exposed to an elderly
stereotype, the college students began to behave more like elderly
adults without even knowing it.

This study was one of the first to demonstrate that our behavior is significantly affected by what we are exposed to, even if the
stereotype to which we have been exposed isn't personally relevant
to us! Since then, this research has been expanded to racial attitudes and behaviors. Many studies have confirmed that our racial
attitudes and behaviors are influenced by our social environment.

One study, conducted by Keith Payne, investigated whether
people automatically associate negative behaviors with black people and positive behaviors with white people, and whether these
racial attitudes lead people to mistakenly perceive a tool as a gun
if it is associated with a black man. Payne and his research team
began by exposing participants to either black or white male faces.
(It is important to point out that the faces flashed on the computer
screen so quickly that participants were unable to say that they
had consciously seen them. But even when we can't consciously
see something, we can still be affected by it.) Immediately after
participants were exposed to either a black or white face, they
were swiftly shown a picture of either a gun or a tool. Unlike the
faces, participants were able to consciously see the gun or tool.

Payne asked participants to determine whether they had just
been presented with a gun or a tool. He observed that when participants had been exposed first to a black face and then to a tool,
they were more likely to mistakenly identify the tool as a gun than

when they were exposed first to a white face and then to a tool. Essentially, this study (and many, many others) demonstrates that the average person in the West automatically associates black men with danger and white men with safety and industriousness.

When I shared the results of this study with my African American brother, he exhaled a weak, pained laugh. "Why would anyone bother to conduct that research?" he asked. "I could have told them that black men are immediately perceived as dangerous."

Black men like my biological brother John and my spiritual brother Drew Hart are telling their painful and prophetic stories, and we would do well to listen to them. As someone who has long studied the ways that racism still bears an imprint on Christianity, I urge you to pay close attention to Drew's eye-opening analysis. In this book, he uncovers the racial histories, attitudes, emotions, and behaviors that have gone undetected in church services, biblical interpretation, and worship songs. He shows that like the college students I described above, many Christians are held hostage to racism without even knowing it.

Let's follow Drew as he leads us on an expedition way below the surface of Christian consciousness, to discover the myriad ways in which we remain captive to racism. I assure you, we're in capable hands.

—*Christena Cleveland, author of* Disunity in Christ,
*director of the Center for Reconciliation,*
*Duke Divinity School*

# 1

# WHEN YOU "FIT THE DESCRIPTION"

After my junior year of college, ten friends and I planned a trip to drive across the country. We attended a Christian college in Pennsylvania, and one of our friends lived in the state of Washington. He lived out in a rural part of the state, and someone had the idea of dropping him off at home and exploring the country by car along the way.

So eleven of us piled into two cars in central Pennsylvania and first headed toward Chicago. We drove leisurely, taking almost a week to get to Washington. We saw Mount Rushmore. We made a stop at Yellowstone, which is apparently a dream destination for many young white adults (who knew?). We stayed at some homes of people we knew along the way, and we camped at campgrounds a few times as well. One night we were behind schedule, so the five of us in my car decided that we'd just sleep in the car rather than set up the tent in the dark. That wasn't necessarily the best night's sleep.

I felt a bit out of place while stopping in some all-white small towns across the country while we traveled. I was pretty certain there weren't any other black people around for hundreds of miles.

But thankfully we had no problems or incidents on the way, and we finally arrived at our friend's house in Washington.

Watching the change of landscapes across the country was unforgettable. But my friend's house was also amazing. The hills were beautiful, appearing for miles like ocean waves. We really were in the middle of nowhere. You couldn't even see a neighbor's house.

It felt like I had truly jumped into an alternate world. We played basketball, football, and Frisbee—because many young white Christians love them some disc! I played piano for the group, and we sang together. We discussed our faith and our deep questions. We were all totally disconnected from our regular, day-to-day concerns.

And then I got a phone call from my mom.

## BLACK IN A WHITE-CONTROLLED WORLD

I have a brother who is one year older than me. For much of my young life we shared a bedroom. We often played and fought together. Others have frequently told me that we look alike. I personally don't see it, though we certainly have similar complexions and builds. We often played basketball together and had a lot of the same interests and experiences growing up. No matter how much we got under each other's skin, as young black men and as brothers, my life was deeply bound up and connected with his.

So there I was, frolicking in the advantages of college life with ten white friends in the middle of nowhere, without a care in the world, when my mom called to tell me about an urgent situation that had developed.

Late one night, my brother was hanging out with friends. They were just minding their business and having a good time. A police car drove by while my brother and his friends were outside and enjoying each other's company.

The cop car drove by again.

Once more the car drove by, but this time the police officers stopped and got out. They immediately arrested my brother for "fitting the description" of someone who had recently committed a crime.

I am still troubled by the lack of description that my brother apparently fit. The only description they had of the guy they were looking for was "black male with a black T-shirt and blue jeans." My brother and his friends were not even at the scene of the crime, nor were they doing anything suspicious at all. But that description was evidently enough for these police officers to arrest and take him to the station.

I later found out that the police also initially claimed that my brother had a bloodstain on his shirt. However, when the lab results came back, they learned that it was just a ketchup stain.

My brother was eventually put into a lineup before the victim in the case. Of course he was not chosen, and finally he was released.

But not before he had spent four months locked up in the county correctional facility.

His crime? Being a young black man in a white-controlled society.

## TROUBLE WE'VE SEEN

Things could have ended up much worse for my brother. I can't exactly call him "lucky," but when black males encounter the police and the judicial system in the United States, things often go very, very badly, whether or not those arrested are guilty. I had always known that being black left one vulnerable in this country, and I certainly had heard about many other black folks dealing with similar or worse situations.

But when my brother, whom many people have said I resemble, was arrested purely based on the description "black male with a black T-shirt and blue jeans," I began to realize how easily something like that could happen to me. Though far worse things happen routinely for black people when going through the judicial process, this event awakened me to the way our nation collectively and quietly accommodates the terrorizing of black people's everyday lives.

Blackness is a visible marker that justifies suspicion, brutality, and confinement by white society. In America, being black has always been defined and understood by the majority group in negative ways: criminal, lazy, obnoxious, ugly, and depraved. White society often deploys static stereotypes and then throws a single blanket over our diverse African American community, denying the beauty and uniqueness of each of us. My brother's experience immediately increased my awareness of my blackness in a country that continues to stigmatize it as a problem to solve. It's not always evident how divided our country is. We are inundated by singing and dancing celebrities, intrigued by suspenseful Thursday nights of scandals and murders, and allegiant to the multibillion-dollar corporations that feed us our sports. With these weapons of mass distraction being deployed, many people ignore the ongoing suffering and the deep racial division that is pervasive and has never gone away. But right below the surface, for four hundred years, deep disagreements about race in America have been boiling.

More recent and publicized events than my brother's arrest continue to expose the deep racial divisions that exist in our country. The United States cycles through event after racialized event, each one sparking outrage over issues of racism in America. For example:

- *Michael Donald.* In 1981, KKK members went searching for any black person and found this nineteen-year-old black male. They attacked him, beat him, slit his throat, and then hung him from a tree by a rope.
- *Rodney King.* In 1991, King was viciously beaten by a group of police officers after a traffic stop. Though they initially claimed no wrongdoing, video was released showing them repeatedly beating and assaulting King with weapons and potentially death-dealing blows.
- *James Byrd Jr.* In 1998, three white men offered Byrd a ride home, then took him to a secluded area where they attacked him, poured paint into his eyes, beat him, and tied a rope around his neck. They then dragged him behind a pickup truck until his body was dismembered.
- *Amadou Diallo.* In 1999, four police officers fired forty-one shots at an unarmed Diallo, whose threat was apparently pulling out a wallet while black. Nineteen of the forty-one bullets struck and killed him. The police officers were acquitted.

- *Sean Bell.* In 2006, during Bell's bachelor party, police officers unleashed a barrage of bullets suited for military combat into Bell's car. One officer alone fired thirty-one times into the car, and Bell and two of his groomsmen were shot fifty times. Neither Bell nor his companions had a gun, as the officer initially claimed. Bell died on the eve of what was to have been his wedding day.

- *Oscar Grant.* In 2009, on New Year's Day, Grant was shot while handcuffed and lying on his stomach at a subway station in Oakland, California. Cell phone videos captured the killing from several different angles, sparking outrage across the country.

- *Aiyana Stanley-Jones.* In May 2010, police entered a Detroit home with guns blazing and recklessly killed Stanley-Jones. She was seven years old and had been asleep.

- *Trayvon Martin.* In February 2012, George Zimmerman racially profiled, stalked, and confronted Martin, a child on his way back to his house after purchasing Skittles for a snack. This led to a physical struggle, which resulted in Martin being shot dead in his own neighborhood. Martin was seventeen years old.

- *Rekia Boyd.* In March 2012, an off-duty police officer recklessly fired several shots into a crowd of people with an unregistered semiautomatic gun. A bullet hit Boyd in the back of the head and killed her.

- *Jordan Davis.* In November 2012, at 7:30 p.m., Davis and some friends made a stop at a gas station. Michael Dunn, a middle-aged white man from out of town, asked them to turn down their rap music, and they refused. Dunn then proceeded to fire several bullets at the car, striking and killing Davis. The police investigation, as well as the testimony of Dunn's girlfriend, countered Dunn's claim that the boys had a gun.

- *Renisha McBride.* In November 2013, following a car accident, McBride went searching for help in the early morning. After she knocked on the door of his house, Theodore Wafer shot McBride in the head with a 12-gauge shotgun through the still-closed screen door. She died immediately.

- *Eric Garner*. In July 2014, a police officer put Eric Garner in a chokehold during an arrest. Garner said "I can't breathe" eleven times before he lost consciousness. He was pronounced dead an hour later.

- *Michael Brown*. In August 2014, in Ferguson, Missouri, a police officer confronted Brown for walking down the middle of the road. Deep disagreements emerged about what followed, with the majority of witnesses testifying that Brown had his hands up while shot, even while the investigation claimed otherwise. The officer fired twelve shots at Brown, hitting him at least six times, including two shots to the head. Brown was unarmed. The officer would later say Brown looked like a "demon" as he approached him.

- *Tamir Rice*. On November 22, 2014, twelve-year-old Tamir Rice was playing with an Airsoft replica gun in a park. Some people called the police to mention their concern, but also said it was most likely a toy gun and that they believed the person to be a juvenile. A police car pulled up to Rice, and within two seconds of getting out of the car, one officer shot Rice in the stomach. Video surveillance shows that officers did not attempt to provide first aid to the boy. He eventually died from the gunshot wound.

- *Walter Scott*. On April 4, 2015, Scott fled from a police officer after a traffic stop and was killed. Initially the officer reported that Scott had stolen his Taser and that he felt threatened. But video footage revealed that Scott was unarmed and running away when the officer shot him five times. The officer had planted the Taser on the ground by Scott's body after he was shot.

- *Freddie Gray*. On April 12, 2015, in Baltimore, Gray was arrested and taken for a long ride in a police vehicle. During that time his spine was severed. As I write this, the details are still not fully known, but an investigation resulted from the uprising that took place after these events. Many ex–police officers have suggested that Freddie Gray was taken on a "rough ride," an unofficial yet routine tactic by which many police officers punish those in their custody.

This list represents just a fraction of the cases that have gone viral in the past few years. Hundreds of people have lost their lives, either through intentional malice or because their lives were not deemed valuable enough to ensure their protection within our white-controlled society. This cycle is not new. It happens like clockwork.

The responses to events like these are also predictable, as many people fall into their default defensive positions. People's perceptions of what happened are as shaped by their socialization as by the event itself. The majority of white people believe that racism is a national problem rather than a problem in their own communities.[1] Many deny and dismiss the experiences of black Americans, claiming that our reactions are mere emotionalism and represent an inability to deal with the facts. Sometimes white people dismiss and label people of color as "race-baiters" for daring to speak on the subject at all. Apparently, only white dominant culture is seeing things objectively and clearly. Everyone else, it is assumed, is allowing outside influences like the media to shape them.

Yet before we think that white supremacy is merely white people's problem, we ought to interrogate how black Christians have been responding to racism in our society as well. While many black churches want to take credit for the civil rights movement in the 1950s and '60s, the truth is that only a small percentage of black churches actually participated in the freedom movement. Few black Christians today have acknowledged how they regularly give their full allegiance to the racialized status quo that slowly destroys us. Many black Christians have partially internalized and reproduced the very same antiblack sentiments and racialized frameworks constructed to subjugate us. Having turned a blind eye to the sufferings of others, too many black Christians, in imitation of the dominant culture, have pursued the American dream in a decisively Western and selfish manner. Too many have rejected following after Jesus concretely and have missed God's revolutionary vision for shalom. While there is certainly a rich

1. Janie Velencia, "Majority Of White People Say There's Racism Everywhere, But Not Around Them," *Huffington Post*, July 7, 2015, http://www.huffingtonpost.com /entry/white-people-racism-poll_55a91a4fe4b0c5f0322d17f2.

tradition of Afro-Christian faith that has resisted the domestication of Jesus for generations, we cannot assume that every black Christian is necessarily joining God in divine transformation and resisting white supremacy through active justice and peacemaking.

Whether white, black, Native American, Hispanic, Middle Eastern, or Asian, we all get caught up in the currents of our white-dominated society and internalize its messages. Each of us must turn to the good news for a more hope-filled present and future. Given the racial history of the church in America, which has unfortunately often been at the center of the problem, few have considered the subversive life of Jesus as the way out of our racialized and hierarchical society.

Churches have often been the least helpful place to discuss racism and our white-dominated society. If racism is talked about at all, it is often addressed on isolated Sundays set apart for grieving some national event or engaging in sparse and limited pulpit swaps. None of those efforts are necessarily problematic. But when our actions are limited to such strategies, they reveal that we don't really understand the full scope or nature of race and racism in our society.

And therein lies the problem. Churches operating out of dominant cultural intuitions, perceptions, assumptions, and experiences define the problem one way, while most black people and other oppressed groups bear witness to an alternative and diverging reality. This epistemological divide concerning racism—that is, the different ways of knowing and understanding life—is an even greater gap within the church than it is among the rest of society.

So what are Christians who participate in dominant society to do when their racial intuitions and racialized experiences contradict the experiences and concerns of historically oppressed groups? Are Christians in dominant culture prepared to listen to groups of people who have seen trouble, so much trouble? Is the church a place where we can talk about the trouble we've seen? Is the church a place not only where we'll be truly heard and understood but also where we will become a transformed community? Will the church take on the form of Christ in our racialized society?

## TIME TO WAKE UP

In the spirit of the original black spiritual, "Nobody Knows the Trouble I've Seen," this book is rooted in what I've seen, in what black people have seen, and in what all who have experienced the underside of white supremacy have seen. This experience from below—from literally living on the underside of America's racial hierarchy—is not commonly known or understood within the dominant culture.

Just trying to start a conversation about racism in the church—which I am determined to do—often results in defensive and even antagonistic dismissals by some of my white brothers and sisters. Having two-way conversations on racism is challenging when white people respond to discomfort with either defensive emotionalism or white fragility, which is the inability to deal with stressful racialized situations. These responses are the norm in too many Christian communities.[2]

The language that dominant-culture Christians frequently use to talk about race, full of colorblind rhetoric, gives the impression that they have somehow transcended these problems. Such claims imply that they do not even notice the diversity of skin tones in people and that they are oblivious to racial categories. However, the common white Christian plea to just "see people as people" is undermined by the highly racialized life of the average white person. White Christians, especially, seem incapable of recognizing the contradictions of their utopian language and their distinctly and deeply racialized lifestyles and daily choices. Colorblind rhetoric prevents people from evaluating the majority of their social relationships, the places they feel they either belong or do not belong, and the kinds of cultural, intellectual, and artistic influences that are worthy of engagement. With such contradictions, I can only assume that it is not color that they are not seeing; rather, it is racism that is being missed.

Colorblind ideology is the twenty-first-century continuation of white Christian silence to racism. During legalized chattel slavery from 1619 to 1865, white silence to this horrific institution didn't

2. Robin DiAngelo, "White Fragility," *International Journal of Critical Pedagogy* 3, no. 3 (2011), http://libjournal.uncg.edu/index.php/ijcp/article/view/249.

get us anywhere. Nor did white silence from 1865 to 1945 move us toward progress. This is the era in which well over one hundred thousand African Americans were forced back into slave-like conditions through the convict leasing system, which allowed people to be arrested for things like not getting permission to change jobs, vagrancy, or perceived inappropriate conduct with a white woman.[3] White Christians were silent when five thousand black men, women, and children were lynched throughout the twentieth century. Many of the early lynchings were actually moments of white entertainment, drawing crowds by the thousands, many of whom took photos of their white children standing in front of hanging black bodies.[4]

From 1970 to the present, the prison system exploded from around three hundred thousand people to over two million. Black males have been most disproportionately affected by the prison industrial complex, most having been convicted for small nonviolent drug charges.[5] In fact, both black and Native American people get shot or abused by police at deeply disproportionate rates compared to the rest of society.[6] Drug use ought to be considered primarily a public health concern rather than seen through the lens of criminality, but the so-called war on drugs has targeted poor black and brown neighborhoods.

Current research, however, reveals that black youth and white youth are using and selling drugs at comparable rates, and yet stereotypes run wild within dominant cultural discourse that make people assume otherwise.[7] As someone who has lived in several black inner-city communities as well as for three years in a white

3. Douglas A. Blackmon, *Slavery by Another Name: The Re-Enslavement of Black Americans from the Civil War to World War II* (New York: Doubleday, 2008), 53–54.

4. James Allen, *Without Sanctuary: Lynching Photography in America* (Santa Fe, NM: Twin Palms, 2000).

5. Michelle Alexander, *The New Jim Crow: Mass Incarceration in the Age of Colorblindness* (New York: The New Press, 2012), 6–8.

6. "Native Americans Get Shot by Cops at an Astonishing Rate," *Mother Jones*, July 15, 2015, http://www.motherjones.com/politics/2015/07/native-americans -getting-shot-police.

7. Alexander, *The New Jim Crow*, 7.

suburban neighborhood, I can personally attest that the war on drugs is not being carried out in white middle-class communities. When white youth use or sell drugs, they are seen as "experimenting" or "going through a stage." When black youth engage in the exact same actions, they are seen as destroying the fabric of American values. This results in our society putting one in every three African American males through the criminal justice system at some point in their lives (mostly for these nonviolent drug offenses).[8] Likewise, black women are the fastest growing demographic being targeted by mass incarceration.[9] The disproportionate policing, stop-and-frisk encounters, arrests, and incarceration of racial minorities ought to awaken the church, because Jesus himself called for us to visit the imprisoned (Matthew 25:34-46) and to bring release to the captives (Luke 4:18-19).

If the response to our racialized society is turning away from and ignoring these outcries rather than dealing with them, how will we ever participate in God's transformational work in a Jesus-shaped way?

The church urgently needs to understand the realities of racism better than it has previously. Christians must do a better job of thinking, analyzing, discussing, and ultimately transforming our racialized lives into antiracist and antihierarchical ways of life that conform to the way of Jesus. We must learn to see and understand the racism all around us so that we can faithfully resist being complicit in its patterns. Once we are able to see it, we must engage in initiatives of deep metanoia, or repentance—initiatives that change us from racialized accommodation to resistance.

## CUP OF SWEET TEA . . . AND RACIAL HIERARCHY

How desperately we need to change our views of racism became distinctly clear to me a few years ago when I met with a white suburban pastor at a McDonald's in the middle of the afternoon. We didn't meet for lunch but just for a beverage that would relieve

---

8. Ibid., 9.
9. "Facts about the Over-Incarceration of Women in the United States," American Civil Liberties Union, https://www.aclu.org/facts-about-over-incarceration-women-united-states.

some of the summer heat. We both decided to grab a one-dollar sweet tea.

I must admit that I find McDonald's sweet tea to be pretty good. It is southern-style. You know that you have had true southern-style sweet tea when you can feel the sugar gritting through your teeth. Yup, it is pure magic.

This pastor was close to my age but a little older, and he pastored a young, white missional congregation outside of Philadelphia. He had reached out to me hoping that we could get to know one another and, more specifically, so that we could dialogue across the racial divide. During our time together we shared lots of stories. We talked about our churches. We discussed seminary life and some mutual professors we have had. We shared some of our personal journeys and meaningful experiences along the way. The conversation was fairly well-rounded. We had some overlapping perspectives as well as diverging experiences and points of views that kept the conversation lively.

And then in the middle of the conversation, this white pastor abruptly grabbed one of the foam cups of sweet tea and placed it directly in the middle of the table between us. It was a sudden and unexpected rupture in the flow of our conversation, and I hadn't a clue what was to follow.

"Drew," he said, "This cup has writing on my side of the cup and a logo on yours." He paused. "But I can't see what is on your side of the cup," he continued. "Likewise, you can't see what is on my side of the cup." This was all happening very quickly, and I wasn't at all sure where he was heading with this teachable moment.

Then it came. "Because I can't see what is on your side of the cup, I need you to share with me your perspective so I can see things from your standpoint," he explained. "Likewise, you need me to share *my* point of view so that you can understand the world from my vantage point."

What a nice sentiment, right? Unfortunately, it is actually a naive way of understanding how racism has perverted human relationships.

So first I expressed my gratitude for his nice gesture. Then I said, "But this is not how things actually work."

I explained that, in fact, I *did* know what was on his side of the cup. This is because I have learned Eurocentric history written from a white perspective. I have read white literature and poetry. I have learned about white musicians and artists. I have had mostly white teachers and professors through every stage of my educational process. I have read lots of white authors and have heard white intellectuals give lectures on a variety of topics. I have been inundated by white-dominated and controlled television and media. I have lived in a mostly white suburban community, and I have lived on a predominately white Christian campus. The truth of the matter is that I wouldn't have been on track to a PhD without becoming intimately familiar with the various ways that white people think. My so-called success means that I have had to know what it takes to meet white standards, whether they are formal or informal.

After explaining why I already knew what was on his side of the cup, I continued on. I noted that in contrast to me, he most likely could go through his entire life without needing to know black literature, black intellectual thought, black wisdom, black art and music, or black history. That is, he could choose to never engage with or be changed by the range and beauty of the black community. Nor would he be penalized for it. That option of white exclusivity would not affect his livelihood or means of providing for his family. No one would question his qualifications if he didn't know how to navigate black communities and cultures or understand the daily realities of most black people in America. Immersion in and understanding of the black community have never been routinely expected or necessary for employees, politicians, scholars, doctors, teachers, or pastors. This is even more so the case for most white Christian communities, which willfully ignore the diverse gifts of the black church tradition. Black faith and tradition are rarely looked to as worthy sources for learning about how to practice spiritual disciplines, embody daily discipleship, and share in Christian community.

This disparity is not merely a result of a fracture in a bridge that divides us racially. That seems to be the way my pastor friend imagined the task necessary to restore human relationships. He seemed, like most people in the church, to comprehend the problem as though it were a horizontal divide between two people on equal standing. If that were the case, then our problem could be fully solved with strategies that mirror cross-cultural exchange programs. We could sit across a table over a drink and swap stories and experiences until we closed the gap of misunderstanding. While cultural intelligence and awareness is definitely needed in these discussions, that horizontal understanding doesn't adequately resolve the full scope of racism in the church or in society.

Racism isn't first and foremost about a horizontal divide; it is a vertically structured hierarchy. Social hierarchy and power have defined, in varying degrees, human worth, beauty, and significance in society. White people since the sixteenth century have been increasingly categorized and perceived to be more valuable, innocent, truthful, and worthy of love and relationship than nonwhite people. Through a paternalistic imagination, racism has taught white people to unconsciously assume that they are the best people to dominate and control society. This racially hierarchical vision, which classifies whiteness as the most prized human characteristic, perceives other people to be at the bottom of the human ladder.

If racism socializes people to overvalue white bodies, as though they were created to rule and dominate over others, then blackness has been conceived as its polar opposite. Blackness in our racialized society has been ascribed with all kinds of negative features, and resides at the bottom of the racial hierarchy. The loss of black life is rarely worth grieving. Black bodies are presumed guilty. Black experience and testimony are assumed to be lies. And experiencing and learning from the range of people and perspectives within the black community is not desirable or needed. Loving black people has never been normative in America.

My white pastor friend had an oversimplified understanding of racism that resulted in an oversimplified solution: two people sit and share stories. Of course such interactions are needed. But such relational engagement and proximity does not necessarily lead toward dismantled racial hierarchies in our lives. Many have thought that pulpit exchanges, multicultural programs, and more conversations with their one black friend would be the solution to racism because they were refusing to segregate themselves for that moment. Such actions may at times align very well with antiracism work, but not always. Very frequently, racial exchange solely happens under the terms and conditions of white people, which in itself is already an act of reaffirming the racialized hierarchy.

Relational, social, and geographic proximity across the racial divide does not necessarily result in the new humanity to which we are called in Christ. One must only remember the close proximity that many enslaved Africans found themselves in during our 250-year history of chattel slavery. This fact reminds us that relational proximity doesn't necessarily dismantle our racialized ideology, intuitions, and behavior. Many enslaved Africans, under the white control of slave masters, frequently labored in the homes of white people. They cooked, cleaned, and raised white children. Many were raped routinely by these overseers as well. This is a deep and intimate proximity, but of course that didn't mean racialized hierarchy was being dismantled in their lives.

Just like my white pastor friend, most Christians tend to operate out of a naive and thin understanding of racism, which doesn't factor in the depth and width of our racialized and hierarchical society. I enjoyed that cup of sweet tea very much, but the analogy of the cup representing two different angles—on equal footing and needing only to be swapped and considered across the racial divide—is insufficient. Without intending to, people who frame racism in this way deeply misunderstand it and its everyday implications. This framework actually prevents people from unveiling the racialized hierarchical society we inhabit.

Hopefully, through a renewed commitment to following Jesus and by pulling back the curtain on racial power dynamics in society, we can transform not only what we know about racism but also how to resist it every day. When we know a little more about racism's impact on society, we can not only bridge the divide of racial segregation but actually begin dismantling racial hierarchy.

## WHERE WE ARE HEADED

Books that rehearse arguments for racial reconciliation have been written several times over. This book will instead guide us through the challenges of racism for the church by confronting Christian frameworks for how racism operates and how it affects our lives. The posture that this book takes as it analyzes racism is one that dares to peer upward at the ladder of racial hierarchy. It looks at the *vertical* expression of power in social relationships, rather than merely sideways across a supposedly *horizontal* gap.

The church must confront its popular definition of racism, which has historically never implicated the white majority by its framing of the problem. Many think that racism is only about KKK-like behavior, or about doing or saying things that were common for white people in the mid-twentieth century. Few have wrestled with what white supremacy—a superiority complex and the practice of racial dominance fueled by racial ideology—looks like in the twenty-first century. Many white people assume racism is only about individual racial prejudice and hatred, and therefore they are always on the lookout for the "bad racists" to scapegoat. Many refuse to think about the larger racialized patterns of society that shape individuals' ideologies and habits. Others assume racism today is just the residue left over from slavery; in their minds, when the older generations die off, we will naturally transition into a post-racial society. These same people have rarely considered the ways that young white people in the twenty-first century continue to make daily choices that advantage them, structurally and systematically, over people who are not white.

My point is that the church's understanding of racism is frequently too thin, narrow, and deficient for it to be antiracist in its witness. Our very instincts about what racism is tend to be unhelpful.

I suggest directly and indirectly throughout this book that our very intuitions cannot be shaped in hierarchy and dominance, as were the postures of Caesar, Herod, and Pilate. Instead, we must come alongside the crucified of the world in solidarity, as Jesus himself did, so that we can have our minds renewed. Dominant cultural intuitions run contrary to Christ's way of knowing. The one taking on the form of Christ in the world does not take for granted the popular or dominant view of things. Rather, the person committed to Jesus follows him to the margins and cracks of society, entering into what I call "counterintuitive solidarity" with the oppressed. Revelation, inspiration, and understanding come in the context of following the crucified Christ in the world.

The book seeks to replace our foundation in the sinking sand of taken-for-granted racialized perspectives found in dominant culture. Instead, it seeks to place our feet on the solid ground and firm footing of the way of Jesus, our Rock. No longer rooted in a world constructed by white supremacist hierarchies and antiblack dehumanizing lenses, we can be formed to withstand the storms and thundering waves of our age. Therefore, the next chapter will immediately begin challenging the shortcomings of commonly held individualistic views on racism, while offering a framework that helps us see our racialized society through widespread patterns and social realities.

Chapter 3 will reconsider the life of Jesus and give attention to the subversive implications of his life and teachings that undermine dominant cultural ways of living. It renounces the image of the white, domesticated, status quo savior that has passed for Jesus Christ for too long. Jesus, the Jewish Messiah executed by imperial Roman methods of torture, now invites us into nonconformity with the racialized hierarchical patterns of this age.

Next, chapter 4 lays out a vital premise of the book: that is, that intuitions shaped by dominant culture are inherently limited. In particular, from a historical perspective, the white majority's way of knowing has repeatedly left it unaware of its own complicity in each generation. Counterintuitive solidarity in the way of Jesus is offered as a revolutionary alternative. Chapter 5 extends those concerns by offering a view into the everyday implications of white identity and practice. In that chapter I will articulate the meaning of whiteness as a social construct and social performance.

Equally important, chapter 6 reflects on the meaning of antiblack racism in society and how it is a problem for everyone, not just for white members of society. This chapter calls us to consider how we all are internalizing the ideologies and habits that affirm and overvalue whiteness as a characteristic above everything else. Black Christians, then, will particularly be challenged to consider whether they actually and concretely love other black people. Here, counterintuitive love, congruent with God's own peculiar love for the least and the last, will gesture us toward sharing love with one another. Once again, in chapter 7, black Christians and other racial minorities will be primarily challenged to consider how the lure of respect and status often entices us away from following the scandalized life of Jesus.

Because this book is largely written from my vantage point, filled with my personal stories as a young black male navigating our racialized society, chapter 8 broadens the scope of social hierarchies and its meaning for other racial minorities beyond the African American community, beginning with Native Americans. Likewise, the chapter reflects on other prominent ways that America organizes society in hierarchical ways through an exploration of the overlaps of race, class, and gender. The church must learn to become attentive to all the diverse experiences within our society. If the church is going to manifest the "beloved community," we must keep track of any time anyone is deemed as less valuable than others. In the spirit of Galatians 3:28, we must renounce all social hierarchies if we are to truly be one in Christ.

Finally, in the last chapter, this book switches gears. In it I move beyond dismantling and deconstructing old and unhelpful frameworks of racism toward offering some everyday practices that will guide the church toward being a people in which the reign of God is visibly manifested. The final chapter gestures toward a communal life capable of subverting white supremacy both internally, in our churches, and externally, in our neighborhoods and around the globe.

When my own brother was arrested and confined in a cage for being a black male, I, like thousands of others, was compelled to wake up and begin speaking truthfully. I was compelled to talk about the racial ladder that has strung people, who are wonderfully and fearfully made, into humanly constructed categories of varying worth.

Join me as we begin to change the way we view racism. "Jesus is the answer for the world today" is not just a cliché. In our racialized and hierarchical society, the way of Jesus is also a realistic, practical way for the church to make the kingdom of God visible.

# 2

# THE RACIALIZED
# SOCIETY I'VE SEEN

Like most people, I have some hometown pride. Norristown, Pennsylvania, is an urban town surrounded by suburban and wealthy neighborhoods and districts in every direction. Full of row homes and historic buildings, Norristown is a town of approximately thirty-four thousand people nestled within Philadelphia's metropolitan boundaries.

Many of Norristown's social patterns conform to the patterns and expectations of communities labeled "urban," especially with regard to above-average poverty levels and gun violence as well as lack of access for many of its inhabitants to quality housing, healthcare, and livable wages. On the other hand, its school district borders are wide, including wealthy suburban neighborhoods on the edges and borders of the borough. This creates a type of economic and racial integration within the school district that is rarely seen in our nation. This racial and ethnic diversity was fertile ground for me to explore society with an open curiosity toward learning more about other people groups. The socioeconomic range of the school district provided space for me to become familiar with racial communities that rarely collide in other geographical contexts.

My hometown uniquely socialized me into a space that contrasts deeply with the experiences of many people in the United States. This place attuned me to see the racialized character of American society, which some people seem incapable of comprehending throughout their entire lives.

My particular block was entirely African American, with the exception of our next-door neighbors, an elderly white couple. Though a soft form of segregation did exist, for young people growing up there it rarely mattered. The further we moved up in grades in the school district, the more we were all funneled together. Lots of elementary schools were situated in various communities, but three middle schools and only one high school served the entire district. This meant that no matter the racial demographics of your block or general area, you inevitably ended up rubbing shoulders with people from other racial groups.

While I lived in Norristown and attended school there, the school district had a pretty serious busing system. (I think it still does.) So instead of attending the elementary school that was literally down the block, I and many other students from my neighborhood were bused out to the more suburban and predominantly white area. There was lots of racial diversity at the school, but nonetheless, I was a minority in elementary school. On the other hand, when I got to middle school, I attended a local school that I walked to each day. Some buses from East and West Norristown (mostly white, middle-class neighborhoods) brought students into our neighborhood. Thus, in these very formative years, I experienced what it is like to be in the majority and in the minority.

Race and class were issues that I had to come to terms with at a young age, though I am certain now that I did so in an unsophisticated fashion. I was forced to take note of how race shaped our community and school. Race and class also played significant roles in housing patterns. If you were white, you most likely lived in middle-class or suburban neighborhoods on the outskirts of Norristown. If you were a person of color, particularly black or Hispanic, you were more likely to live in Norristown proper, in a particular set of neighborhoods. These were not hard lines of segregation, so there were lots exceptions. Yet the pattern was still visible enough for one to notice.

Likewise, our middle school had a tracking system, which was supposed to cluster similarly academically inclined students based on their academic performance. The top tracks, however, were almost exclusively white. The rest of Eisenhower Middle School, and particularly the lower tracks in the system, darkened dramatically.

I was placed in one of the lower tracks in middle school. The few unfortunate white students who got trapped down with the rest of us were also exceptions to the rule that dictated that white students were in the top tier. My sister consistently performed at high standards in school and found herself also being an exception to the rule. She was often the only black student in her mostly white classes. She still reminisces about that experience. Through that tracking system, she often ended up in deep friendships with Asian students in Norristown who also tended to get tracked for success.

Norristown as a whole was not a cleanly segregated community. Many of my white peers also lived within the borough of Norristown. In that sense we were very multiracial, and the divisions often seemed to fall along class lines as much as racial ones. However, at the time I was not able to ask why we as African Americans were historically more likely to be poorer than the majority of our white peers.

I felt incredibly ordinary and average in middle school and early high school. Of course I had the insecurities that all preteens and early teens have, but I also blended in well. I wasn't the most popular kid, nor was I the outcast. I rocked to Heavy D and Nas, sported my Starter jacket, and cried when both Biggie and Tupac were shot and killed. I loved Friday mornings at school. This was because we would always talk about what happened during Thursday night's episode of *New York Undercover*. (Sorry, Mom and Dad, but we always snuck it in when we should have been asleep.) I loved basketball. Many of the guys in the neighborhood enjoyed basketball and football. When everyone else left the court for a game of football, I would stay on the basketball court and practice

by myself. I not only played, watched, and talked about basketball
but also had an extensive card collection and was always looking
for a good trade when I went to school. This all seemed normal.
I certainly didn't think deeply about what it meant to be a young
black male in Norristown, at least not at that age.

Certainly the tracking systems and the residential patterns
alone suggest that blackness meant something in Norristown, but
I rarely sensed my presence being perceived as an overt threat.
The occasional white clerk would follow me around in a store,
but I hardly cared. I was oblivious to the ways my body could be
perceived as a danger or threat to white people—as I would later
in life see more clearly. I felt regular and average in Norristown.

As life continued to unfold, however, this sense of normalcy
soon lost all meaning.

## WHEN BLACK IS SUDDENLY COOL

My life drastically shifted when I was fourteen years old and our
house caught fire while we were at a Sunday evening church service. Having lost almost everything, our six-member family briefly
relocated to a small, three-bedroom apartment for the rest of the
school year. My dad had also recently become the senior pastor
at Montco Bible Fellowship, an African American church located
outside of Philadelphia in a predominately white suburb. The natural move, then, was to relocate closer to the church. This meant,
for my siblings and me, moving into the North Penn School District and attending a high school with three thousand students
from tenth through twelfth grade.

The idea of moving to the North Penn area terrified me. All I
could imagine was a school filled with white kids sporting green
Mohawks and riding skateboards, or white cliques full of football
jocks and cheerleaders. Clearly I had watched too many cheesy
1980s television shows and movies. I actually had nightmares
about how I would be received there. I just knew that I would get
picked on as the black kid. I was convinced that other students
would not like me and that it was going to be a rough experience.

Sometimes our perceptions, however, are far from the reality.
To my surprise, being black and male didn't make me a target

for bullying in my new high school. Being black and male meant instant popularity.

Don't misunderstand me: I'm not saying racial stereotypes weren't running rampant. The place was dripping with them. But the racial stereotypes tended to boost my popularity rather than stigmatize me as an unwelcomed "other." Black male stereotypes at this suburban school apparently were in style. I didn't have to work to be accepted, and kids frequently tried to befriend me.

I can still remember my first few trips to the basketball courts after moving to my new school. Team captains consistently picked me early on to be on their teams—sometimes I was the first chosen—even when no one had ever seen me play before. They just assumed that I could play ball (which I could and loved). They also assumed that I loved hip-hop (which again was right, though not usually the particular rappers they most enjoyed). Even though most kids knew little to nothing about my personality or character, I was constantly given instant credibility. I quickly realized something. While in Norristown I had generally been seen as an average kid (though clearly with low racialized expectations of my future), something magical was happening in this white suburban space: my body was looked upon and instantly assumed to be cool.

I hadn't changed between Norristown and North Penn. I had the same body, character, and personality. The only difference was that this area had drenched itself in romanticized black stereotypes—ultimately still negative ones, despite the social affirmation I received. Blackness translated through racialized gazes in this community meant coolness, athleticism, and being a "bad boy."

I came to North Penn High School expecting that I wouldn't be accepted because of racist stereotypes that would lead people to think they knew who I was before they actually got to know me. Instead, I found a community that *did* accept me, in a way, but only because it was full of racial stereotypes that led people to assume they knew me. The racial gaze upon my black body certainly was there, but it frequently looked very different than what I expected.

I was just beginning to learn how complex racism was, and that it could be manifested very differently in various communities and regions.

## WELCOME TO WHITE CHRISTIAN COMMUNITY

Toward the end of my time in high school, I began sensing a call to ministry. Or to state it more honestly, I finally stopped ignoring the sense of calling that I had had for a while. So I decided to enroll at an in-state Christian college far enough away from home (about a two-hour drive) to give me a certain sense of independence, yet close enough that I could get home on breaks and vacations.

I was fully aware that this college was mostly white—it had even less diversity than North Penn—but I wasn't concerned. Why should I be? My logic was pretty simple: I had already experienced being a minority at a mostly white school in the Philly 'burbs, and that was a *public* school. But at college I'd be among my brothers and sisters in Christ, which meant we would have a much closer bond. I figured it would be a breeze. I believed not only that I would be able to handle being a minority at a Christian college, but also that I would thrive while there.

This belief—that I would be deeply accepted and treated as an equal within a mostly white Christian community—proved to be a large miscalculation. In fact, looking back, I think it was probably the most naive expectation of my entire life. My first two weeks in the dorm left me feeling sick to the stomach because of the cultural isolation. There were very few other African American first-year students, which meant that I was the only African American on my entire floor in the dorm. I quickly discovered the whole different world that you experience when you live in close quarters with people who have unfamiliar cultural inclinations. The music people listened to seemed strange and unfamiliar, and some of it seemed to me to be very dark and troubling. Most of the TV shows and movies students routinely referenced were not on my radar. And while other first-year students were quickly building relationships, I found myself, for the first time in my life, feeling like I just didn't belong at all.

Despite a slow start during those first few weeks, I remained very friendly and outgoing. I reached out and eventually built strong relationships with many people, especially in the dorm. Before I knew it, I had become one of the more "popular" folks on the floor. Everyone loved them some Drew. If there was a movie to be watched, it was in my room. If there was a prank to be pulled, I was orchestrating the procedure masterfully. (During my sophomore year, my nickname was "the Godfather"—no joke.) I was, if anything, overly outgoing.

During my first couple of years, I didn't discuss race a lot with my peers, at least not in any serious fashion. I mostly engaged in race humor to cope with feeling so isolated and so conscious of my black body in such a white space. I joked about my big black fridge, my black microwave, and any other black appliances I had that I felt were superior to other people's appliances. It was dumb, but that is how I coped.

But subtle racialized situations that I had initially ignored began to overwhelm me. At times it felt like a continual and ongoing assault. People on campus who had not yet gotten to know me personally responded to me very differently from those with whom I had developed a relationship. I saw the discomfort or suspicion of my presence from many students. When I surveyed the campus at a distance, people seemed very friendly and smiley. But when I walked down the main walkway through campus, many people would move to the edge of the sidewalk and look down or away as they passed by. I saw a pattern in which students primarily did this around me and other people of color. I saw people's posture change in an odd way when I joined in group conversations where everyone present didn't know who I was. To be fair, though, I didn't notice this behavior at first. It is only after you have seen it for the hundredth and thousandth time that its recurrence becomes clear as day.

And then there were the comments. People made horrific comments about black students on campus, including some students who routinely referred to all the black males on campus as "thugs" and "troublemakers." I overheard white students insinuating that being on the basketball team was the only reason that most of the black male students were accepted to the school in the first place. Black female students also experienced constant slights, from cultural ignorance and insensitivity, overt stereotypes, and inappropriate touching. In particular, I remember many of the black women on campus talked about people constantly touching their hair without permission. Also, any sign of confidence and assertiveness was always articulated as being rude, angry, disruptive, and out of place. In contrast, the confidence of many white male students on campus, as I observed it, tended to be much more prominent and on display. But their confidence never yielded these types of responses. Black women on campus were more likely to get treated as though they were invisible, in contrast to the hypervisibility that many black males experienced.

As if that were not enough, the campus atmosphere often highlighted African American culture only to have it mocked by both insensitive students and even a small handful of faculty members. I will never forget the denigration of the gospel choir, particularly from a white faculty member whom a black female student overheard saying that the gospel genre wasn't "real music." With that coming from a faculty member, it was no surprise then that some students used our sincere worship music as an opportunity to publicly mimic expressive worship styles during chapel. It was as if they thought the music was supposed to be for humor and games rather than for praise and worship of God.

What pushed things over the top for me was when I started to catch some folks within my own circles making comments about other students of color—people they did not know personally but who were friends of mine. Some of these white friends of mine would pull out the old "you are different from them" rhetoric. It was as if our friendship had no bearing on breaking their stereotypes of other black students at all. In their racial framework, I was the exception to the rule that allowed them to gaze at other black students as thugs or charity cases. They must not have even thought that there was a possibility that the way they were socialized to see black people was distorted, or that their racial lenses were the actual problem rather than black and brown students. The reality was that I was no different than the students of color to whom they were comparing me. In fact, one white peer of mine once called a black male student and the rest of his friends "thugs." The target of his character assassination happened to be one of my close, lifelong friends—a guy that I had grown up with since middle school.

Those experiences would forever change how I interacted within homogeneous white Christian spaces. The ongoing racial prejudice on campus was more persistent and life-draining than anything I had seen in my life. Nothing, including the black church I had grown up in, had prepared me for white Christian community. I was becoming cynical and at times very bitter about the church and its racism. I sometimes shared my experiences with white students on campus, but most did not take my words very seriously. I had to deeply recalibrate my social networks based on these experiences just so I could make it through. Each little cut, on its own, was insubstantial. But by the end of my time in college, I found myself with a thousand paper cuts that hurt like hell.

At the same time, I had the privilege of majoring in biblical studies. Through classes and conversations in my department, my eyes were opened to how Jesus identified and stood in solidarity with vulnerable women, ethnic Samaritan outcasts, the poor, and the systemically excluded and oppressed. I studied how the prophets called God's people back to lives that practiced justice and mercy. I saw that central to understanding Paul's letters was seeing his particular calling to form reconciled communities composed of Jews and Gentiles gathered around the Messiah. And probably more than anything, I was challenged to read Scripture in a way that truly took Jesus seriously by studying his life and teachings and by believing that we are actually supposed to conform our own way of life after his. My theology professors introduced me to a range of books that gave me some language to name the problems of American Christianity, like *Divided by Faith*, *Myths America Lives By*, and *Mere Discipleship*.[1] Basically, I was given a biblical and theological framework to address the social failures of the church in America, which had never been presented to me so clearly.

---

1. Michael Emerson, *Divided by Faith: Evangelical Religion and the Problem of Race in America* (New York: Oxford University Press, 2000); Richard Hughes, *Myths America Lives By* (Urbana: University of Illinois Press, 2003); Lee C. Camp, *Mere Discipleship: Radical Christianity in a Rebellious World* (Grand Rapids, MI: Brazos Press, 2003).

By my senior year, I was a serious vocal dissenter to the racism on campus. You couldn't be friends with me and not hear about the racism that plagued our campus. I started finding my voice, and I made sure that the students were aware of the issues and concerns that many black and brown students were experiencing on campus. I also began to check up on some of the younger black students on campus who were adjusting to life on campus, to make sure they were doing well.

I can still remember a conversation I had with a black female student a couple of weeks before her graduation. When I casually asked her, "How ya doin'?" she immediately broke down crying. She had experienced a racially offensive incident in recent weeks, and was deeply troubled by how it all went down. She declared aloud to me that she never wanted to step foot on that campus again after her graduation. She said that if she could, she would pack her luggage so she could drag it across the stage with her as she got her diploma. That way she could leave right for the car and never look back. I don't know if she still feels as strongly about her experience on campus, but she had been deeply wounded during her time there and couldn't wait for it all to end.

As I reflect on my college experience, I'm left with the fact that this mostly white Christian college was a more racially hostile and antagonistic space than Norristown, in which different racial and economic groups had their lives structured together. It was also more difficult and draining for me than the mostly white suburban public school. How could that be? How could my time among white Christians have been more painful for me as a young black male than my time among white non-Christians?

I am grateful that I was a biblical studies major throughout this season of my life. I was being stretched in my Christian journey further than I had been before. I developed a broader understanding of the biblical narrative, of the prophetic tradition, of the meaning of Jesus' life and teachings, and of the new humanity that broke the hostility between Jew and Gentile. This was a needed intervention for me, helping me better articulate why Jesus was the answer to all the issues I was experiencing. Even though my Christian community didn't reflect this new way of life, I gained a vision of God who, in Jesus Christ, is unfolding true justice and shalom.

## BLACK BODY, RACIALIZED SOCIETY

Now, through hindsight, I am able to look back on my formative experiences from middle school to college. Now I am positioned to see how my black body was always navigating a racialized society and being interpreted by white onlookers, but in very different ways. In Norristown I was able to feel comfortable in my body, without being self-conscious about what others thought about me. I didn't feel a sense of hypervisibility, nor did I feel like I didn't belong or as though I was an "other." Yet Norristown was still a very racialized space and still very hierarchically structured. Race and class mixed in a complex fashion but always in a manner that found black people disproportionately poor in comparison to white peers. And the tracking system systemically and structurally proclaimed the continuation of the status quo: that white people hold positions of advantage even when they are the minority in a community, and black bodies are still disproportionately lodged at the bottom of the ladder.

While I was able to navigate my hometown and feel normal, my body's presence meant something completely different when I transferred to the large white suburban public school system outside of Philly. There I instantaneously became cool. I had the same personality, same talents and gifts, same good looks. But now, through a white, suburban gaze, somehow I was made anew while not changing a thing. I was now navigating a space that romanticized blackness as the "cool other." Yet with this unearned coolness projected onto my body also came a full package of stereotypes. People believed they knew everything about me before they even got to know me.

Finally, my body made the leap once again, but now into a mostly white, Christian space. There I was neither "normal" nor the essence of coolness. I had somehow been reinterpreted as a "threatening other." Once again many white people thought they knew me, but it wasn't in a manner that instantaneously led to friendships. (I had to work for that.) Instead, the white Christian gaze most often interpreted my black male body as that of a thug. That was the way I felt people reacting to me, and that was the precise language I heard white students use to describe other black students they didn't know very well or at all.

Through struggling to make sense of my body's constant reinterpretation by a white gaze, I learned that race always means *something* in our society. During my last year of college, two white female friends, on separate occasions, each confessed to me that they had been afraid of me when they first met me. I hadn't known specifically that they felt like this, but I had seen this fear more broadly in how other students interacted with me. After having known me for four years, my friends each told me how silly this fear now seemed. I was actually relieved to hear my dear friends share this with me. I received those words in love. My only desire for them was that they would not let me be an individual exception in an ongoing pattern of seeing people through a racialized gaze. I hoped that they would go on to interrogate their assumptions about all the other black people they encounter.

## THE RACE CARD AND THE RACIALIZED DECK

I would be rich if I got money for every time a white person told me that I was playing the race card. It has happened frequently, and at times that have really surprised me. The accusation that I am playing the race card rarely comes from people who have patiently dialogued with me. Rather, it comes from people who, right from the beginning of the conversation, dismiss my perspective rather than considering whether my views might help them enhance their own.

Merely speaking about a particular incident *and* mentioning racism often results in the accusation of playing this mythical card. This criticism—that one is "playing the race card"—is impulsively used over and over to stigmatize those who disagree with the myth that America is now a colorblind, post-racial nation. This is a script that even white Christians seem to have learned and rehearsed. Rather than remaining open to the stories and experiences of people who have been historically oppressed, people in dominant culture frequently employ cliché phrases that begin with dismissal and encourage willful denial. The possibility for mutual transformation is cut off when we don't at least remain open while listening to dissenting perspectives in society. The status quo path in America, and often for the church, is avoidance of all in-depth considerations of systemic racism.

White and black Christians seem to find racism at very different moments and believe it to flow in very different directions. Sometimes it is permissible to point out overtly racist individual situations, though white listeners will often deny that the event was racist unless it was extremely overt and particularly hateful. It is much more acceptable in America to talk extensively about reverse racism. *Reverse racism* is the term developed by white dominant culture to suggest that the real problem of racism today is that white people experience prejudice and discrimination by people of color. According to this framing, white men have it the hardest right now in our society. Despite the fact that white men are overrepresented and predominant in the state, economic, religious, political, and media sectors, within the reverse racism framework, they are the true victims in the American story.

I have often gotten frustrated by the many little remarks that dismiss black experiences. But I decided at some point that I was going to play along with the rhetorical "race card" game.

This is how the game works. Some racial incident, such as the shooting of Trayvon Martin by George Zimmerman, occurs. A large percentage of white Americans interpret the event from a particular cultural and social vantage point, while African Americans interpret that same moment very differently, in light of their own experiences, history, and context.

We'll say that each incident is interpreted by "playing a card": that is, choosing an interpretation of the event that seems most fitting and insightful. In the case of Trayvon Martin, I "played a card" in chapter 1 when I described how George Zimmerman racially profiled and followed a minor solely because he was black, a behavior that led to a physical altercation and the murder of that child. So that would be "the race card." A "card," then, is an isolated event. "Playing a card" simply means stating one's interpretation of that particular incident. Every incident—every moment in which we are racially divided on what happened—is followed up with playing a card—that is, interpreting what happened during the divisive moment.

African Americans, having experienced hundreds of years of racialized oppression as a community, often look at particular incidents in particular ways. Through the lens of their experiences, they recognize the continuity of systemic oppression, which has merely mutated shape and form, and along the way their analysis often becomes rather sophisticated and structural in nature. In this way, they say that a particular situation is racist and needs to be addressed.

The moment that racism is brought into the conversation, however, many from the white majority label this move as "playing the race card." By doing so, they suggest that race is being brought up inappropriately. The *wrong* card is being played, they suggest. For example, this claim is reflected by many who assert that there was no racial element in Michael Brown being shot and killed in Ferguson, Missouri. At the heart of the accusation that someone is "playing the race card" is the suggestion that African American interpretation of an event is unduly subjective or has been manipulated.

There is a long history, going all the way back to slavery, of white Americans not trusting black perspectives as truthful. Therefore white verification is required to confirm every black thought and testimony, because on their own they hold no weight in court or public opinion. White perception is assumed to be more accurate and objective than black perception.[2] Because she or he has categorized an event as racial in nature, the African American speaker must be called out and dismissed.

What I would like to suggest is this: white folks are the only ones considering a single card. White people typically are obsessed with interpreting the meaning of *individual cards*, or incidents. They look at the isolated card and then judge it by their whims and assumptions, which (no surprise) rarely ever find white people to be racist. For four hundred years, in any given era, the white

2. Yolanda Pierce, "When Our Truths Are Ignored: Proslavery Theology's Legacy," *Religion and Politics*, August 10, 2015, http://religionandpolitics.org/2015/08/10/when-our-truths-are-ignored-proslavery-theologys-legacy/.

dominant group has always created a definition for their generation that absolved them from charges of wrongdoing and racism while reaffirming their innocence amid ongoing white domination and control over society and further racial oppression. The white dominant standard of racial discernment rarely finds white racism, while simultaneously deciding that the specific card played was falsely made into a "race card." An individual moment, event, or action is judged by looking for KKK rhetoric, or maybe the N-word, or some cross burning in the yard. If such overt hate crimes prominent in the early and mid-twentieth century are not currently present or visible, then the racial component of the complaint is quickly dismissed.

Unlike the dominant culture's tunnel vision that focuses on one card, the black community is usually considering the *entire deck*— that is, ongoing history and current widespread social patterns. We have laid out all the cards in front of us on the table. Rather than zooming in on one card, we have zoomed out to look at all the cards laid out together. All of a sudden, just like in any deck, you begin to observe patterns: four aces, four kings, four queens, and four jacks. Our definition of racism is not based on a definition that dominant society both has created and continues to wield to deny any wrongdoing. No, we refuse to "play their game," even if we work with their cards.

Instead, it is only after looking at the reoccurring patterns, studying the whole pack, and then gathering the entire deck and putting it back in order that we claim to make sense of any individual card. We aren't playing the race card; we are analyzing the racialized deck.

It is this very act—the careful and patient observation of systemic racial components of our society—that the majority of white America has refused to engage in. Choosing to trust their own intuitions and personal, subjective assessments—which are socialized in dominant culture—many white Americans focus on an individual card rather than attempt to make sense of how that card fits into the larger deck.

So you want to play cards? Well, let's fix the rules of the game and recognize that black people aren't playing the race card.

Typically, dominant society has been consumed by a single card while most people in the African American community have been working with the entire racialized deck. And what we have always known is that the deck is stacked against us.

## DEFINITIONS OF RACE AND RACISM

*Race* and *racism* are commonly misunderstood terms. Despite its common usage, race is not a natural biological category for human beings, though physical features certainly create boundaries of difference. The language of race obscures rather than clarifies human similarity and difference. It is smoke and mirrors. Instead of being a biological fact, race is a social construct. Racial categories are not inevitable; they were created—and not very long ago, given the length of human history. And while human prejudice between competing people groups is ancient in practice, race and racism are not.

Most people live as though race were an essential biological category that properly differentiates between types of people—or else they pretend that race doesn't exist at all. Some people think that because race is socially constructed it can best be eradicated by denying its existence. The logic at first may seem tight. And if there weren't centuries of impact on oppressed groups, compounded by current racialized systems of injustice, denial of race might actually be a reasonable solution.

Although race is a lie white people invented that divides humanity into categories used to oppress nonwhite people, the concept has created tangible people groups. These groups have felt, and continue to feel, how very real all of this has become. Race is a social construct that not only shapes how we perceive particular people groups but also justifies oppressive hierarchy and European domination over nonwhite people. Leading critical race theorists Michael Omi and Howard Winant unpack this idea further:

> Although the concept of race invokes seemingly biological based human characteristics (so-called phenotypes), selection of these particular human features for purposes of racial signification is always and necessarily a social and historical process. Indeed, the categories employed to differentiate

among human beings along racial lines reveal themselves, upon serious examination, to be at best imprecise, and at worst completely arbitrary. They may be arbitrary, but they are not meaningless. Race is strategic; race does ideological and political work.[3]

We should never separate race from its ideological and political work. The global practices of European domination, colonization, and conquest in the Americas and Africa in the sixteenth century required ideological justification. Otherwise, such brutal and inhumane practices against indigenous communities would undermine Anglo-Saxon Protestants' image of themselves as an innocent Christian nation. Drawing from an older, preexisting myth of Anglo-Saxon superiority, white supremacy and racism constructed a white-dominated understanding of the world rooted in racial hierarchy.[4] Combined with the fact that each Western nation believed that they were the "New Israel" and therefore had divine rights to rule, this myth resulted in a deadly reality for those on the underside.

So although *race* may indeed be socially constructed, that does not mean that *racism* is imaginary. It is very real. Some 12.5 million Africans were shackled and brought across the Atlantic Ocean because of racism. From the seventeenth century until 1865, generation after generation, Africans were enslaved, whipped, raped, tortured, and executed because of racism. Lynching and Jim Crow and white terrorism in the twentieth century happened because racism is real. A specific and particular community has been racially discriminated against under the category of "black." With precision, white Americans have engaged in redlining, white flight, economic exclusion, and educational disparity, all of which are trends with racialized features and racist outcomes.

The ways that most people articulate racism don't consider its development, purpose, and most importantly, how it has structured society and human relations. The dictionary definition of racism is usually insufficient. It is the common, taken-for-granted,

3. Michael Omi and Howard Winant, *Racial Formation in the United States*, 3rd ed. (New York: Routledge, 2014), 110–11.
4. Kelly Brown Douglas, *Stand Your Ground: Black Bodies and the Justice of God* (Maryknoll, NY: Orbis Books, 2015), 4–23.

dominant cultural definition. It is solely based on how the white majority and dominant culture define and discuss race and racism. Some fail to realize that the dictionary operates like a mirror, merely reflecting how we already commonly use language. The dictionary's definition of a particular term does not mean it is the most insightful use of a term; it is just a commonly understood way of using it. Just as *google* and *selfie* have become verbs in many current English dictionaries, because those have become mainstream uses of those terms, so too has *racism* been defined by its common usage in most dictionaries.

At the heart of it, *racism*, from this dominant cultural vantage point, is defined as "personal prejudice or hatred of someone of a different race." Of course, such an intention-based definition is extremely hard to prove. How can you prove what someone believes deep down, on the individual level? We might at times have a strong sense that something is wrong, and might even be confident of someone's prejudice because that person uses overt racial language. But ultimately, someone's heart is not measurable in the scientific sense. This definition of racism actually protects both those who operate out of racial bias consciously and those who operate out of racial bias unconsciously, because they can always deny it. Furthermore, it turns our attention away from the way that our entire society is a racialized system. We must rid ourselves of this definition because it leaves us with nothing but subjective assessments of individual moments, in which people or incidents are rarely assumed to be racist. In fact, the only time that American dominant culture accepts accusations of racism is in cases of so-called reverse discrimination. According to many white people, then and only then can this thin definition of racism be applied with certainty and without proof.

There is another definition of racism, however, and it comes from the sociology department rather than English dictionaries. Specifically, in a field of study called critical race theory, racism is explored and analyzed as a social phenomenon. Critical race theory asks a particular set of questions: What is the meaning of race in a society? How is society organized by race? What are the origins of racism, and how does it operate in and affect our daily lives?

In this view, *racism* is "a racialized systemic and structural system that organizes our society." Racism structures society in such a way that the white dominant group systemically advantages and overvalues its own group members while oppressing and exploiting other people. All of this seems justified because of the dehumanizing categories and ideologies designed to make an "other" out of nonwhite people and because of the "legitimate" and "official" channels through which policy is enforced.

When we look at the racialized patterns of society, both historical and sociological, we begin to grasp a problem bigger than individual prejudice. Through a consideration of widespread and ongoing social realities, we can see that America has always been a highly racialized society, one dominated and controlled by a white majority. Sociologist Joe Feagin asserts that "today, most major U.S. institutions remain, mostly or disproportionately, white-male-controlled in their normative structures and white male in terms of those who hold the top decision making positions."[5] These racialized and racist patterns are easily discovered once we know what to keep track of.

With a sociological framework, we can begin to see that the average white person lives a highly racialized life, though he or she is often unaware of it. Patterns of self-segregation become clear. One lives mostly among those of the same race. The same thing goes for one's church, intimate relational networks, phone contacts, and guests at the dinner table. You can even see the racial distinctiveness of most people's bookshelves, social media contacts, and music. Through these social patterns, sociologists are able to reveal high levels of self-segregation among white Americans (more so, on average, than among black Americans).[6]

---

5. Joe R. Feagin, *Racist America: Roots, Current Realities, and Future Reparations*, 3rd ed. (New York: Routledge, 2014), 33.
6. On self-segregation among white Americans, see Robert P. Jones, "Self-Segregation: Why It's So Hard for Whites to Understand Ferguson," *Atlantic*, August 21, 2014, http://www.theatlantic.com/national/archive/2014/08/self-segregation-why-its -hard-for-whites-to-understand-ferguson/378928/; on self-segregation among black Americans, see Christopher Ingraham, "Three Quarters of Whites Don't Have Any Non-White Friends," *Washington Post*, August 25, 2014, http://www.washington post.com/news/wonkblog/wp/2014/08/25/three-quarters-of-whites-dont-have-any -non-white-friends/.

These patterns also begin to reveal what it means to live on the underside of our racialized society. Take note of the racialized patterns and common experiences of too many black people all over the country, such as being profiled or brutalized in their communities by police. Digging up, searching for, and compiling all of these realities helps us make sense of a widespread social problem that is not just about one individual moment.

This perspective suggests that naming any moment appropriately first requires seeing these broader patterns. People must first be able to understand the patterns of the deck before they can understand the meaning of one individual card. Interpreting a racially divisive situation without knowing the history and current social patterns and without hearing a wide range of stories throughout the community is like trying to compete on NBC's show *The Voice* while only playing an air guitar. It just doesn't work. We must get familiar with the entire deck first before we turn back to making sense of an individual card.

This perspective on racism requires that people in the dominant culture have deep and wide conversations with the black community. Typically, many white people search for the one black person who holds the same positions and perspectives as they do, and then prop that person up as verification of their own beliefs. Taking a riskier and more teachable posture—allowing an entire community to speak into their lives—would ultimately result in changing their operating definitions. White people must learn to define individual incidents in light of the larger pattern of society.

When we can be honest about how our entire society is deeply racialized, we will be ready to move forward. Racial moments are the norm rather than the exception. What is spectacular? It's the individuals who buck the racialized system by resisting it, rather than unknowingly being socialized and determined by dominant group norms. To resist naming our racialized society is to create an unfair game in which players, according to these rules, must never try to connect the dots between widespread patterns and individual events. Of course, in the community of truth and grace, we resist any denial of historical and contemporary systemic oppressions in society. We take the time to understand the experiences of communities living on the underside of our society.

## OUR CULTURAL REFLEXES AND BAD RACISTS

In 2013, celebrity chef Paula Deen made some really ugly comments. News came out into the public square that at one point in her life, Deen considered having a southern plantation–style wedding, with all black servers. She also admitted having used the N-word. Deen ended the whole circus with an awkward confession from a black employee that she was not a racist. And Deen then attempted to express how close this black male employee was to her; because she had a black friend (though it certainly didn't seem like a relationship at all), of course she couldn't be racist.

America was not buying it. Deen's racism was too overt, and she broke all the rules. She used what we could call "old-school racism," which is no longer acceptable in the public square, instead of "new school racism," which has shifted its rhetoric to fit the times. Americans of almost all backgrounds and classes wagged their fingers at this woman in disgust. You could almost hear everyone thinking, "Bad Paula Deen!"

Well, guess what? Pointing to Deen's racially offensive words was not particularly spectacular or courageous. Rather, it was the expected response within America's twenty-first-century context.

Don't get me wrong. I am not going to defend Paula Deen in the slightest. That would be absurd! I am not suggesting that we consider her comments anything other than racist ideology and speech. All I am suggesting is this: the scapegoating of Paula Deen is the sophisticated cultural reflex of a highly racialized society that doesn't want to own up to how racism works systemically.

Consider this: the greatest threat to black life is not Paula Deen calling someone "nigger." Rather, it is the white supremacy embedded into systems within our country, advantaging some people at the direct expense of others. It is the racialized and inequitable public school systems, the war on young black people (known as the "war on drugs"), the mass incarceration of people of color, and the lack of adequate housing and access to living-wage jobs. It is the systematic practice of white preference in social networking and the preferential treatment of white people for employment regardless of qualifications. (This is the case even while some people simultaneously complain about the unfairness of affirmative action—which, in truth, has mostly benefited white women rather than black people.[7])

It is not Paula Deen's pitiful but individual ideology that is most harmful; it is the entire racialized society that is sick and that ignores the daily welfare of people who are of African descent. In fact, Paula Deen can only come to be and think as she does within a society like ours.

When we point the finger at Paula Deen, we misdirect all of our attention to one small, isolated symptom of a much bigger root problem. I hope that we can begin to redirect the focus back to an entire people group that has benefited from an economy built on stolen labor and stolen land and that continues to apathetically oppress Native Americans and black people.

The magic of it all is that racial oppression in the twenty-first century has become so sophisticated and subtle, in contrast to the overt racism in the mid-twentieth century, that no one even realizes that they are complicit in the system or that their own hands are dirty. One out of three African American males will go through the judicial system at some point in their lives because they have been categorized as a danger and a problem by the white dominant group. Young black women and men cannot drive their cars or walk on the streets of their own neighborhoods without being disproportionately more at risk of dying at the hands of police.

So long as the white majority is mostly fine, not having dirtied their hands directly, they can claim innocence while pointing the finger at blatantly racist ideology from the Paula Deens of the world. The noise surrounding these overt moments, compared to the silence around the more devastating racialized systems destroying black people, is deafening. Who cares about holding Paula Deen responsible if we refuse to do anything about the sophisticated racial oppression that produces people like her a hundredfold every day?

---

7. Jessie Daniels, "White Women and Affirmative Action: Prime Beneficiaries and Opponents," *RacismReview* (blog), March 11, 2015, http://www.racismreview.com /blog/2014/03/11/white-women-affirmative-action/.

Paula Deen didn't drop out of the sky, nor did she create these racialized ideologies on her own. She is not that slick. No. These ideologies were passed down from hundreds of years of white supremacy and, more specifically, handed to her through living communities that affected her. When mainstream America makes an example of Paula Deen, it both turns her into a scapegoat and also creatively claims its own innocence, because it limits the definition of racism to individual acts. In doing so, the dominant culture washes its hands of all the racial ideology that it permits, the racialized injustice it ignores, and the racialized patterns of life in which it participates. If you want to hold Deen accountable, then let us also hold the entire racialized system accountable for its calculated violence against black, Native, and brown life.

Our society is structured by a racialized hierarchy that results in racial gazes. These racial gazes can operate differently in different spaces. My personal experience, especially during my undergraduate years, is that the white Christian community has the most intense racialized spaces and gazes. If we are to better interpret racialized situations and moments, we must begin to look for widespread patterns through history and society and to listen attentively to the voices of those at the bottom of the racial hierarchy in America.

As we will see next, Jesus lived a subversive life under the hierarchy of Rome and the Jewish authorities, who were complicit in the ongoing domination. And Jesus still offers his disciples a way forward as we navigate our racialized society today.

# 3

# LEAVING BEHIND THE WHITENED JESUS

On Sunday mornings when I was little, I would run down the steps into the kitchen while wearing my Sunday best. According to my mom, I'd be wearing my "church clothes," including my sharp clip-on tie. When I made my appearance, gripping my Bible in my hand, I would loudly proclaim to everyone (which was the small audience of my family) a bold message. I would say, in my best minister's voice, "The preachings of the gospel! The preachings of the gospel!"

My grandfather was the preacher I came up under in church back in those days. I admired his bold and confident preaching. I too wanted to preach the gospel. At that point, however, I was only beginning to understand what the gospel really is.

Only through a long journey would I discover that the gospel is much more comprehensive, subversive, dangerous, and even undermining of everything that I knew and took for granted in life. It is a divine intervention in history and a life-altering reality. God descended and was revealed in the birth, life, teachings, death, and resurrection of Jesus, and it is in this same one that all things are sustained and through whom all things are being reconciled. The gospel is about Jesus.

God is not a taken-for-granted idea or proposition that we can comprehend just by being socialized in a supposedly "Christian" nation. God does not fit into our box. Our finite assumptions about God are mere projections of our own wanting. For this reason, God has been commonly thought of as an old white man in the American imagination. And Jesus also was remade through white supremacist imagination into the likeness of a white man with distinctively Anglo-Saxon features and Western culture. In 1967, Vincent Harding articulated the effect of a white American Christ on not only white churches but black churches as well:

> From the outset, almost everywhere we blacks have met him in this land, this Christ was painted white and pink, blond and blue-eyed—and not only in white churches but in black churches as well. Millions of black children had the picture of this pseudo-Nazarene burned into their memory. The books, the windows, and paintings, the filmstrips all affirmed the same message—a message of shame. This Christ shamed us by his pigmentation, so obviously not our own. He condemned us for our blackness, for our flat noses, for our kinky hair, for our power, our strange power of expressing emotion in singing and shouting and dancing. He was sedate, so genteel, so white. And as soon as we were able, many of us tried to be like him.[1]

Jesus was revealed in Matthew, Mark, Luke, and John; was testified about by Sojourner Truth and Henry McNeal Turner; and is uniquely present among the least, the last, and the lost of our society. And the gospel of Jesus is manifested visibly by kingdom citizens who have disciplined their bodies and have been formed by the Spirit after the image and likeness of Christ. Our descriptions of Jesus ought to be consistent with his revelation in Scripture. And what we find both in Scripture and by watching those who have sought to truly live as Jesus lived (1 John 2:6) is that Jesus' way is very subversive.

---

1. Vincent Harding, "Black Power and the American Christ," The King Center Digital Archive, http://www.thekingcenter.org/archive/document/black-power-and-american-christ#.

As Christians, we have developed all kinds of fancy theological tricks and justifications that allow us to circumvent Jesus as recorded in Scripture. We don't think it's necessary to immerse ourselves in the gospel narratives so long as we call on Jesus' name. We are not concerned that the Jesus we follow sometimes bears more similarity and likeness to Uncle Sam or ourselves, in thought and reasoning, than to the crucified Messiah in Christian Scripture. Of course, we all are shaped by our culture, and all see dimly, but at times there seems to be no resemblance between "our Jesus" and the apostolic and scriptural witness we have. Jesus may be our answer, but our projections of Jesus may also be our problem.

When considering the racial problems in the United States, we must begin taking the New Testament Jesus more seriously, in all of his subversive and troubling implications for our social order. Howard Thurman recognized these problems decades ago, in the mid-twentieth century. Thurman reminded his readers that Jesus was Jewish rather than a white man, poor rather than some wealthy elite, and part of an oppressed minority living under occupation rather than one domineering over others in the sociopolitical realm. Jesus was among "the disinherited," an obvious feature of the Jesus story for those open to seeing and hearing.[2] After we discard the white, elite, Western Jesus, a human construct used for sociopolitical domination, we open ourselves up to the divine revelation of the poor, oppressed, Jewish, and ultimately crucified Messiah. And in a life of discipleship, we will find the way that can dismantle and dis-align the racial hierarchy and order upon which our lives are built.

Racial hierarchy didn't exist in Jesus' day, but he navigated a society built upon other forms of hierarchical power, particularly as it related to ethnicity, gender, class, and other realities that intersected with Roman imperial occupation and the religious political establishment in Jerusalem. Jesus was always concerned with how society left vulnerable people as stigmatized social outcasts. Jesus subverted these hierarchical forces and categories that dehumanized people as though they were lower on a human ladder of value

---

2. Howard Thurman, *Jesus and the Disinherited* (New York: Abingdon-Cokesbury Press, 1949).

and worth. Rediscovering the subversive Jesus, and his life amid social hierarchy, will reveal to us God's divine presence and activity in the world today.

## UNDERSIDE OF THE UNDERSIDE

Born in Bethlehem, Jesus had a humble beginning. His company was not Caesar, nor Pilate, and certainly not Herod. The audience to the great moment of his birth, beyond his parents, was shepherds. These were the undesirable and despised underclass of society.

Shepherds lived life on the margins. These weren't the cute Christmas card or Sunday school program shepherds. During this time, Rome was the ruling empire over the Jews, and consequently all of Israel understood what it meant to be oppressed—what it meant to live life with someone's foot against your neck. The Jews despised their Roman occupiers and desperately wanted to see them kicked out of their land. The Jews were oppressed, exploited, and humiliated. And yet, when we understand the social class of shepherds, we remember that they themselves, among their own people, were further stigmatized and unwanted, seen as misfits and left living on the margins of society. They lived on the underside of the underside. What God would make an arrival with people at the bottom of the social hierarchy, as if they were the preferred crowd?

Simultaneously, Caesar Augustus, the Roman emperor, made a decree that had the whole empire registering for taxes. Pure and simple, this was economic exploitation of an occupied people. Augustus had consolidated the Roman Empire, taking hold of centralized power over the boundaries of his reign. He also claimed that his adopted father, Julius Caesar, was divine after he passed away. Audaciously, Augustus also began to refer to himself as "a son of god," believing his own press that he somehow brought peace and justice to the world through his might. The emperor was believed to be at the very top of the Roman imperial hierarchy.

Ironically, with all of his centralized power, political domination, and exploitation of others, the emperor was still clueless about what was actually taking place on the ground in the little town of Bethlehem. God was in the midst of enacting a history-altering moment. Jesus was soon to become an unstoppable force that not even the most powerful empire in the world could contain. The incarnational (God taking on flesh) entrance of Christ was off the grid. He was able to "steal away" into the metaphorical "hush harbor" of Galilee.[3]

Caesar's imperial life at the top of the social ladder actually *distanced* him from what God had done on the margins in the person of Jesus. Despite imposing a registration and census of all the people in his empire, he still didn't have a clue about Jesus' birth. He would never see Jesus face-to-face. Caesar's kingdom was hierarchical and run from the top down, but Jesus' kingdom centralized the outcasts on the margins from the bottom up. In essence, the one who attempted to occupy the center had actually placed himself on the margins of God's restorative and liberating activity in the world. And the one born on the margins was actually at the center of God's shalom erupting into our groaning creation. Jesus' birth gestures toward a God nothing like Caesar.

This good news went first to the marginalized shepherds. It was a life-changing announcement that was going to alter everything. This was a message that brings hope to the poor, uplifts the brokenhearted, revitalizes the tired, liberates the oppressed, and declares that God's kingdom has arrived.

What was the good news that was shared? It was that on that day a Savior, a deliverer, a liberator was born in the city of David. He was the Messiah, the awaited king of Israel who was prophesied about in the Scriptures. This Messiah, or Christ, was the true Lord. Counterfeit lords who demanded ultimate allegiance would soon be unveiled as frauds and fakes.

Also, notice the sign given to identify Jesus as the Messiah. The angels told the shepherds that they would find Jesus, the King of kings and Lord of lords, lying in a feeding trough for animals. He wouldn't be identified as Messiah because of some royal procession; he wouldn't be identified as Christ for being born in a

---

3. "Hush harbors" or "brush arbors" refer to the secret gathering places of enslaved Africans, as they would come together to worship God in spirit and truth outside of the watchful eye of white supremacist surveillance.

palace; he wouldn't be identified as God's Son because of a royal announcement given from Rome. No. Instead, he would be recognized for being born in some little town out in the country, lying in a humble feeding trough. None of this divine activity was accidental. The very location and circumstance of Christ's birth was a symbol and sign of God's solidarity with the socially oppressed and outcast. It bears witness to Paul's claim that "God chose what is low and despised in the world, what is regarded as nothing, to set aside what is regarded as something" (1 Corinthians 1:28). This is the precise way God chose to reveal God's self to the world, demonstrating a deep identification with the majority of the world who struggle with dehumanizing poverty and oppression under dominating forces. Jesus' birth in the manger was a visible protest against the powers of this world that denigrate the dispossessed.

According to Matthew, things didn't settle down for Jesus as a young boy, either. In fact, life was increasingly unsettling. His family had to flee because Herod was carrying out a genocidal campaign against his young peers. Jesus' family became refugees on the run. They were displaced immigrants hiding out in Africa for safety. He would eventually move back and be raised in Nazareth, in the middle of Galilee, when it became safe again. But nonetheless he was born on the wrong side of the tracks. People asked, "What good can come out of Nazareth?"

Jesus' life is particularly significant given his subversive invitation to his followers to be formed after him. In his life and ministry, Jesus found solidarity with the poor, with the oppressed, with vulnerable women, with the socially rejected and marginalized, with ethnic Samaritan outcasts, with the demon-possessed, and with the blind or physically sick. A Jew himself, his daily life was primarily among the masses suffering under the occupation of Rome. He regularly confronted and frustrated the local religious leaders, claiming to have ultimate authority even over the Mosaic Law itself, which sounded fairly blasphemous, because only God could have that authority. He protected those charged with sexual sin from the punishment of the religious leaders, shared life intimately with tax collectors and violent insurrectionists, and invited each of them to follow him into new life.

The kind of life that Jesus lived was grassroots and subversive, traveling from town to town with his improper and scandalous crew. Jesus' kingdom ministry was disruptive to the social order and therefore a direct threat to the social, political, religious, and economic establishment. His life and ministry undermined the powers, yet without ever swinging a sword.

## THE SUBVERSIVE WAY OF JESUS

In Luke 13, Jesus had been traveling through various towns and villages, teaching about the kingdom of God and calling people to repent and to follow him. He was busy healing the sick and restoring the outcast so they could fully participate in society, affirming their dignity as humans loved by God. Suddenly, according to Scripture, some Pharisees came to Jesus. Unlike the stereotype of Pharisees as hypocrites, which commonly circulates in the church, we see that in reality Jesus and the Pharisees shared the same social world. Much of their conflict came from differences exposed by proximity.

Therefore, these Pharisees quickly approached Jesus, warning him, "Get away from here, because Herod wants to kill you" (Luke 13:31). Herod was basically a thug king who had been put in place as a puppet of the empire to keep the Jews in that region in their place. The Jews were so difficult to control because their submission to God conflicted with Roman allegiance. Nonetheless, Herod's hierarchical reign over others was threatened by Jesus' presence. Herod was intimidated, as he should have been, by this bottom-up kingdom of God, which was radically reordering all social relationships. And it was gaining traction right under his nose.

Herod's death threat helps put some perspective on how subversive Jesus actually was. In the gospel narratives, Jesus' crucifixion is not a random, one-time characteristic of his life. Jesus' entire way of life reveals him consistently clashing with the status quo establishment in such a provocative way that various powerful and well-connected people were always wanting to kill him. Jesus' subversive life placed him in constant danger by those who ran society.

As I already mentioned, Jesus' presence was so threatening that we are told in Matthew that Herod not only tried to kill him but also committed genocide of countless young boys in the process, forcing Jesus' family to flee for their lives. Furthermore, Jesus' first sermon, recorded in Luke 4, wouldn't be described exactly as a home run by the standards of most American Christians. Actually, he started off well. He began by talking about how justice and liberation were about to be experienced because the day of Jubilee had come through him. This is the liberating moment when slaves are emancipated, debts are forgiven, and land is restored. All these things level the playing field and flatten the social hierarchy.

That message wasn't a problem. Jesus' oppressed Jewish audience was with him there, and they understood Scripture's implications for justice. But then, instead of collecting the offering and saying the benediction while he still had the crowd in the palm of his hand, Jesus continued on to explain that the boundaries of God's activity and favor extended beyond Israel to Gentiles as well. The Jews were a covenant people so they could be a blessing to the nations, not so they could be an exclusively favored people before God. God has always been present and active among Gentiles, especially scandalized and marginalized ones.

The crowd did not like Jesus challenging their script of how they understood themselves before God, so they tried to throw him off a cliff. According to John 10:22-39, things got really bad for Jesus. The religious leaders wanted to seize and stone him. They asked Jesus to be up front about whether he was the Messiah. Jesus, however, said that his very deeds testified to who he was and that they nonetheless still did not believe. Of course, after Jesus claimed that he and the Father are one, these leaders became furious with such seemingly blasphemous words, and they picked up stones and once again wanted to kill him. But he escaped their clutches.

Of course, this is not a comprehensive list of the ways Jesus threatened the establishment of his day. There are other times when people wanted or threatened to kill Jesus according to the Scriptures. My point is that Christ's actual crucifixion was not the only time that Jesus' life was in danger. What is clear from these few examples is that the life of Jesus was so subversive and radical that he repeatedly undermined and clashed with the status quo establishment. These clashes inevitably and repeatedly resulted in people wanting Jesus dead. Jesus did not affirm the existing social order. And there is no doubt that today Jesus also identifies with black men and women experiencing the daily threat of police brutality—especially those who, like Jesus, have courageously resisted the establishment upholding the racialized status quo.

Luke 13 tells us next that the Pharisees told Jesus to "get away from here" (Luke 13:31). Their intuitive reasoning was probably that Jesus ought not to risk continuing with such subversive ministry in that region, where the backlash for his radical way of life might catch up to him. Instead, Jesus boldly headed right for Jerusalem—a place, as Jesus explained, known for executing people sent by God. Jesus understood his revolutionary ministry to be on the border where God's disruptive kingdom and the old social order of domination collide. And he did not avoid that calling in an effort to live a comfortable and secure life. Subversively, he remained steadfast.

In response, Jesus sent these Pharisees back to Herod with a personally worded message, beginning with this precise phrase: "Go and tell that fox" (Luke 13:32). Yes, you heard that right. Jesus engaged in some radical, revolutionary, and very defiant speech. He clearly didn't respect Herod, a Roman puppet ruling over the Jews. And just so there is no confusion with our English usage of this word and its meaning for that time: Jesus was not playing nice. When Jesus called Herod a fox, he wasn't complimenting him for being sly and sharp. Nor did he find Herod cute or sexy. No, Jesus defiantly dared to tell the truth to Herod about his role in a blasphemous empire that claimed to be a savior to the world to justify its conquests and military expansion. In Jewish literature, there were three ways that the term *fox* was commonly used, other than in reference to the actual animal. First was to call someone a predator, because foxes hunt for their food. Second, somewhat like calling someone sly, Jewish literature also used the term to describe someone as a deceptive person. Third, foxes are small animals, so calling someone a fox could be a way of saying that person was small or insignificant.

It seems like any or all three of these options could fit this scenario. In any case, Jesus took up the radical prophetic task of speaking God's truth to a powerful person who was lording over his community. He symbolically named and unveiled this violent and unjust man. In naming him "that fox," Jesus unveiled Herod's true character and role in things. He was a puppet for the violent, oppressive, and blasphemous Roman Empire, which had aligned its way with evil forces contrary to God's reign on earth.

Jesus was defiant and determined to continue manifesting his subversive kingdom right within and under the jurisdiction of the powers until he clashed with the establishment in Jerusalem. His resolve was that "nevertheless I must go on my way" (Luke 13:33). He would not be turned around. A similar sentiment was expressed in the 1960s when the people sang that they wouldn't let anyone "turn us around." Jesus was on a mission. As his disciples living in a racialized society, we must reenvision what types of prophetic words need to be spoken in our day to unveil the hidden evil forces of oppression and hierarchy, which have been permissible in our society for too long.

## TWO WAYS OF LIFE

This Luke passage presents two ways of life, each clashing with the other in how it organized community and wielded power. Where the old order structured life by wielding its coercive power to take life, intimidating the masses into subjugation, Jesus' kingdom reconfigured life around the authority of God, taking down thrones, casting out demons, healing the sick, feeding the hungry, liberating the oppressed, and proclaiming good news to the poor. Where the old order dominated and violently lorded over others, the kingdom of God arose from the bottom, margins, and cracks of society, freely inviting people to share in the peace and justice of God made available in the presence of Jesus. The old order called people to be puppets for the status quo, while God's kingdom liberated people to discover who they truly were. And while participating in God's kingdom, people found that they were created in the image of the Maker of heaven and earth.

The kingdom of God has become visible right under the surveillance of those who claim supremacy over others through control and domination. These contrasting ways of life offer different promises, different ways of life, and different end goals. The old order is passing away, and the kingdom of God is the future that God has for us that has been ushered into the present. The kingdom of God is already being experienced, in part, right now, for those who are willing to follow and cling to the delivering presence of the living Jesus.

In this story Jesus also expresses that on the "third day" he will "complete" his work (Luke 13:32). Of course, the third-day reference, for us as the church, becomes a not-so-subtle reminder of Jesus' resurrection. The resurrection of Jesus is a game changer. Without victory over sin, death, and the forces of this world, and without the promise of experiencing the world to come with Jesus, following after him and participating in his rejection and suffering seem illogical. Yet with the resurrection, death has lost its sting. That is why Paul talks about Jesus in this way: "Disarming the rulers and authorities, he has made a public disgrace of them, triumphing over them by the cross" (Colossians 2:15). We are reminded that Jesus is victorious over the cross itself, triumphing over all the social, political, and spiritual forces that aligned together in hopes of destroying him. And we don't have to fear when we join Jesus' revolutionary movement. We will also participate in Jesus' resurrection.

And yet there can be no honest understanding of resurrection outside of a world of crucifixion and death. Jesus, consequently, insists that "it is impossible that a prophet should be killed outside Jerusalem" (Luke 13:33). Jesus is heading straight toward Jerusalem. He has been stirring up a different kind of revolution, one not predicated on hierarchical violence. Jesus has started a kingdom rebellion in which his citizens love their enemies, redistribute their resources justly, forgive one another, treat the poor with dignity, live in solidarity with the vulnerable, and liberate the oppressed, all because they worship and praise the God of Jubilee who has been revealed. Jesus is prepared for a big confrontation, even as he already knows what the result will be. The death-wielding, evil forces of the Jerusalem establishment will put their full weight against him, in hopes of destroying him and his movement.

In response to the cycle of violence from Jerusalem, Jesus laments. He cries out, "O Jerusalem, Jerusalem" (Luke 13:34). He is emotionally tugged by the life and trajectory of Jerusalem, in relation to both its leaders and its inhabitants, who suffer under Roman occupation. Both are caught up in destructive cycles of violence, having bought into the logic that violence rather peacemaking would ultimately bring shalom and God's kingdom into existence. It is important to remember that the word *Jerusalem* actually means "city of peace" or "city of shalom." It was intended to be a place that made visible God's reign. But instead of being an alternative social order manifesting God's shalom, it was acting just like the rest of the world, seeking violence as the answer, including against God's prophets. Both Herod and Jerusalem represent the ways that a religious people can become accommodating of, complicit in, and implicated by the sinful and violent ways of the empire. Knowing all of this, Jesus is still undeterred. He is determined to carry out his covenant mission as the suffering servant to the nations, accepting the consequences in his own body for providing deliverance to the nations.

Just when Jesus seems to not be able to get any more revolutionary, he returns to the usage of animal-centered stories to make some serious social analogies about his society and its failed ethics. People often seem to resort to symbols, and particularly animal figures, when they desire to say otherwise extremely hard-to-hear things. For example, enslaved Africans in America used the Brer Rabbit stories to powerfully critique slave society, and yet they did so without it resulting in their immediate death. Death certainly would have occurred had they made those same critiques without such creativity and prophetic imagination. The book of Revelation also does this significantly, although I know there is a lot of debate around the meaning and purpose of such symbols. This kind of storytelling lends itself to being a tool for the underdog of society. It creates space for subversive speech that reveals realities that have been hidden and covered up.

Jesus begins to talk about his desire for Israel as his children, and how he longs to gather them like a hen gathers and protects its chicks under its wings. This forces us to confront two different animals in this passage, each representing very different ways of being in the world. They are two contrasting ways of life. The first, as we already discussed, is the fox. The fox is a predator; it is deceptive, but it is ultimately just a small figure. The fox is a puppet for greater, bigger actors. The fox's way of life is violence. It wields death, and its end is death.

The hen, in contrast, is motivated by a deep and courageous love for its children, its chicks. Out of such motherly love, it is willing to endure the brunt of the attacks of the fox in attempt to provide cover and safety for its chicks. It longs to create a life-giving space of flourishing and shalom under its wings and within its realm. But if the chicks go running in every direction except toward the hen, then they have chosen to experience the full brunt of the vicious cycle of violence and destruction outside of the hen's wings.

According to Jesus in Luke, Jerusalem was unwilling to look to the Prince of Peace and would thus be forsaken and unprotected. Thereby Jerusalem would be left vulnerable under the whims and brutalities of the Roman oppressors. As historians of first-century Palestine can tell you, this is more than just a parable. In the Gospels, Jesus predicted multiple times what was going to happen to Jerusalem if people refused to take up the way of Jesus by following his subversive life of transformation and peacemaking while caring for the most vulnerable in society. In Luke 19:42, Jesus is less cryptic, and once again laments over Jerusalem because residents didn't know "the things that make for peace"; he suggests that such a path meant that their enemies were going to surround them and crush them. And by AD 70, Jerusalem was literally destroyed by the Roman Empire. Over six thousand people were crucified. Thousands and thousands more killed. The entire city was leveled to the ground. When Jesus said, "Your house is forsaken" (Luke 13:35), he was referring to the absence of shalom that would be experienced. This had direct physical, social, and political implications. This illustration of the hen and its chicks wasn't a warm, fuzzy message. It was a prophetic warning about God's people living counter to what God was doing on earth as manifested in Jesus Christ. It was a warning about being complicit in, as well as crushed under, imperial power and violence.

Jesus follows that by saying, "You will not see me until you say, 'Blessed is the one who comes in the name of the Lord!'" (Luke 13:35). Most of his listeners would have been anticipating a visitation from God as Jeremiah prophesied, and many would have also expected a messiah who would come and deliver them from their unrighteous oppressors. This would happen in Jerusalem. Yet when the time came, they did not recognize God in the flesh.

Isn't that something? They could not recognize that it was God manifested in Jesus. They attended synagogue and observed the torah their whole lives. Yet when God took on human flesh, somehow Jesus looked nothing like many people's projections of the divine one. We now know that if you want to know what God looks like, then look no further than Jesus Christ. He is the revelation of the triune God in bodily form. Jesus is the clearest image we have of God.

## CHRIST CRUCIFIED

God becoming one of the crucified ones of the world is baffling. It goes against the way we conceive of God in the world. If most American Christians were told to think of a pyramid of power and to place Caesar and God on it, they would almost certainly elevate Caesar above most people. Caesar had a lot of power. We think of him as shaping history and running things. Most Christians would also insist that God is at the top of the pyramid of power—in fact, so far at the top that it would make Caesar's power look insignificant and ridiculous.

Yet have we really grasped the meaning of God's power if we simply think that divine power is just a supersized, Caesar-like power? Isn't that merely the taken-for-granted logic of a society that refuses to meaningfully understand the revelation of the crucified Christ?

In 1 Corinthians 1, Paul sets aside the sensible, informed, and enlightened perspectives of God that existed during his time. He is not impressed with human wisdom. He asks, "Where is the wise man?" (1 Corinthians 1:20). For Paul, human wisdom cannot compare to God's wisdom. In comparison, human wisdom is nothing but foolishness. God's wisdom is expressed most vividly in the crucified Christ. This is a stumbling block for some and just plain foolishness to others. God's Messiah, who suffered and was crucified by an oppressive power, is the key that unlocks a new way of exploring society in a truer way.

Not only is the *wisdom* of God unlocked in view of Christ's crucifixion but so also is the *power* of God. Let's come back to my discussion on the idea of a pyramid of power. The problem with thinking about God's power as imperial power on steroids is that it doesn't consider God's power expressed in the crucified Christ (1 Corinthians 1:24-25). Paul forces us to ask, "What kind of power is this?" The truth is that God's power is not like Caesar's power! It is a different kind of power. God's way of doing things looks nothing like Caesar's. Divine power isn't beating earthly rulers and authorities at their own tyrannical game; rather, God undermines and subverts their power in a way that to us looks very much like earthly weakness.

What kind of God is this? That God has been revealed as a crucified liberator from Galilee should dismantle our earthly conceptions of divine wisdom and power. The American god of dominant culture seems foolish and weak once we realize that God has chosen to especially restore, liberate, reconcile, and transform our world from below. This God dwells among the socially vulnerable and marginalized, who have always been discounted by the dominating and controlling group in society.

## IMMERSED IN THE SUBVERSIVE LIFE OF JESUS

Americans in great numbers have passionately cried out "Lord, Lord" every Sunday. Likewise, there is no question that America has a long, horrific, four-hundred-year history of white-dominated, racialized practices including slavery, white terrorism, lynching, Jim Crow segregation, humiliation, police brutality, mass incarceration, inequitable educational and economic opportunities, and much more. That Christian piety and oppression could so easily coexist should be horrifying. It can happen, though, because the Jesus being referred to in America rarely had any resemblance to the subversive life embodied in the gospel narratives of Scripture. Rather than creating a new order, the American god has too often been the sustainer of this old order, white supremacy and all. The god passed down from generation to generation in dominant culture legitimized our racialized hierarchy. People have assumed that white American "old-time religion" was synonymous with the kind of religion that God accepts (James 1:27). Taking for granted that God is with them, most people grow up always presuming what God is like. Many intuitively believe that God blesses America and thinks of it as a divine vehicle in the world. God's America is (or was) mostly an innocent Christian nation. We can throw out clichés like "God is sovereign," "God is all-knowing," "God is [fill in the blank]" because we have God in our doctrinal box. Unfortunately, dominant cultural reflections on God rarely adhere with the revelation of Jesus as specifically attested to in Scripture.

Dietrich Bonhoeffer, while in prison before being executed for following Jesus into resistance of the white supremacist regime in Germany, addressed the same concern.

> Everything we may with some good reason expect or beg of God is to be found in Jesus Christ. What we imagine a God could and should do—the God of Jesus Christ has nothing to do with all that. We must immerse ourselves again and again, for a long time and quite calmly, in Jesus's life, his sayings, actions, suffering, and dying in order to recognize what God promises and fulfills. What is certain is that we may always live aware that God is near and present with us and that this life is an utterly new life for us; that there is nothing that is impossible for us anymore because there is nothing that is impossible for God; that no earthly power can touch us without God's will, and that danger and urgent need can only drive us closer to God.[4]

---

4. Dietrich Bonhoeffer, *Letters and Papers from Prison*, Dietrich Bonhoeffer Works, vol. 8 (Minneapolis: Fortress Press, 2010), 514–15.

For too long, the church has gone about its business as though nothing were wrong. Meanwhile, it has been a racialized organism, not only fractured relationally but actually practicing, perpetuating, or remaining silent to the racial oppression of others. And yet Jesus, in his birth, life, teachings, death, and resurrection, has been the answer available to us all along. According to our sacred Scripture, Jesus lived a life that nonviolently subverted the powers and confronted the establishment. The wisdom and power of God, of a different sort from earthly wisdom and power, is something we are invited to participate in as God's church. We are the called-out ones—not from the world, but from being patterned by the wisdom and power of this world through our sinful practices and mind-sets.

Jesus can help us transform how we understand and resist racism in our society. Through the Holy Spirit, Jesus can help us participate in God's presence in the world rather than perpetuate racism unknowingly. We must consider how American Christianity's common sense has failed to understand the world from the perspective of crucified Christ. In the next chapter we will consider the limitations of white dominant cultural ways of knowing, and will seek a more Jesus-shaped posture from which to view race and racism in our society.

# 4

# DON'T GO WITH YOUR GUT

Since graduating from college in 2004, I have traveled all over the United States to speak at churches, conferences, colleges, and seminaries about racism and the church and about the way forward that Jesus provides. On one particular occasion I was speaking at a building that has roots going all the way back to the oldest Mennonite congregation in America, founded in 1683. Located in the Germantown neighborhood in Philadelphia, this place had special meaning for me, because in the year 1688 members from this community signed the first written antislavery document. Therefore I saw it as an honor to deliver a lecture on race, racism, and the church from within the walls of this historic building.

After my talk and the subsequent question and answer session, I lingered for a while so that I could talk with attendees. An older white gentleman approached me and wanted to chat with me about my talk. He began by expressing his deep gratitude for everything that I had shared that night, but then he made an interesting comment that seemed to contradict his previous statement. He said that he agreed with 95 percent of what I said, except for my interpretation of what happened to Trayvon Martin. This talk occurred right in the middle of a tense racial division in our country, exposing that we could not come together and agree that what happened to this boy was wrong. For this gentleman, all of my analysis of the history of race and racism was right on the money. But when that same lens was applied to a current issue, we seemed to fall back to square one.

I left this event with mixed feelings. I was well received there, but I struggled to understand how someone really could agree with the larger historical narrative I gave and then continue to read this specific instance in contrary fashion. This man, as far as I could tell, had good intentions and wanted to be against racism. While I have certainly encountered some people who have gotten really defensive or nasty, most people I have met are like this man, truly wanting to be part of the solution. Most people want to contribute constructively to dismantling the racial division that exists.

Although that is a great start, I've come to realize that is not enough. Even with that goal, I've seen the ways in which Christians continue to be deeply divided, particularly in their perceptions of racism in America, and seemingly unable to understand counter positions. When racial animosity explodes in our country, as it has in recent years in Ferguson, New York City, Baltimore, and Charleston, we are forced to talk about racism more publicly. When that happens, we find ourselves once again face-to-face with this stark reality: we do not even agree about what is going on, let alone what should be done about it.

To make any progress in understanding each other across racial lines, we in the church must begin to talk about our own socialization, which we have received from various communities. We need to wrestle with *where* our opinions have been shaped. Despite the fact that we might think that we came up with our own thoughts and perspectives, all ideas are developed in particular contexts and spaces. We are all socialized in some way, because we have all been part of real human communities. Communities and cultures shape us. These cultures partly shape our values, worldviews, and everyday norms and practices. Our ideas and assumptions do not just drop straight from heaven; nor do we develop them completely on our own, as though we are lone rangers in our intellectual development. No, each of us comes from somewhere (or from multiple contexts), and each of us has been deeply shaped by these contexts. We can choose whether to take those things for granted or to critically receive them. Are we willing to wrestle, over and over again, with what we will keep, what we will discard, and what needs some adjustment?

What I want to consider in this chapter is how this very act of unwittingly accepting the dominant cultural view of things, especially as it relates to race, cripples our conversations on racism in the church. At a more basic level, relying on "intuition," which is actually formed by our racialized social contexts, has led many Christians to faulty understandings of racial dynamics. Many dominant-culture Christians never even imagine that they might need to interrogate their own intuitive responses to racism.

To break the cycle of ignorance to racism and faulty intuition, members of dominant groups must learn to *not trust their own gut*, as they have been socialized outside of the life experiences of marginalized groups. Instead, they must follow our Lord, Jesus Christ, who in his own day stood in solidarity with Samaritan outcasts, vulnerable women, the hungry, poor, and the socially rejected.

These points suggest that there are different ways of knowing, and it is our task to explore and pursue Jesus-shaped ways of knowing our world. Could it be that the social place in which we stand ought to be as close as possible to that of Christ's own life? Could it be that we would then see the world more truly and more clearly than we currently do?

## WHAT IS SOCIALIZATION?

African Americans, as well as other people of color who have had to navigate life as minorities, often accept the reality that they have been socialized. Cultural socialization is much easier to understand and recognize when your way of doing things is constantly labeled and differentiated, and often mocked. When your traditions, wisdom, stories, and values are constantly scrutinized or pointed out, it is not hard to see that you have been raised in a distinct cultural context.

For white Americans, however, and anyone who has been part of a dominant culture around the globe, dominant-group socialization is normally not as obvious. Those living as part of a majority, dominant culture are less likely to be conscious of their own socialization. Rather than thinking of their own lives as being shaped by a peculiar context or culture, people who constitute the majority of a society are often unconscious of these realities. Individualistic frameworks prevent people from seeing that their viewpoints are not quite as original as they would like to believe.

Many white Americans tend to think that everyone else is "cultural" or "ethnic." They view themselves as just "average Americans" or "normal." This is especially the case the more racially segregated one's life is, because one's own culture determines the norm and is thereby preferred in the public square, in local institutions and schools, and among peer networks. In such contexts, it's not hard for people to blindly take for granted the racial character and particularity of their own social formation. They rarely have to think about it.

I can remember many times that white people have said to me things like "I don't have a culture" or "I'm just a 'normal' American." They assume that their interpretations of the world are the purely objective and universal perspectives that everyone else should adopt. Not being conscious of one's own cultural socialization can lead to thinking that one's perspective is not just *a* vantage point but *the* vantage point. Not recognizing that everyone has been socialized by society quickly results in assuming that our way is the right way, and hence God's way. In America, the white dominant cultural way is often assumed to be the right way. The culture, values, and norms of the dominant group get translated into the universally right and moral way of life.

And therein lies the problem. White intuition, perception, assumptions, and experience—limited by homogeneous networks and socialized in dominant society—claim one thing, while black experience claims an alternative and diverging reality. This epistemological divide—that is, the partition between our different ways of knowing and perceiving—is an even greater reality in the church than among the rest of society.

To understand this, we must peek at various historical moments in America's past, leading up to the present, and consider how the dominant group in America has been blinded by the ugly realities of the society of which they have been a part.

## WHITE DOMINANT CULTURAL INTUITION IN AMERICA'S PAST

Throughout most of American history, the majority of white Americans, having been socialized by the values and perspectives of the majority culture, didn't think we had a racial problem. The white community has hidden its own hand from itself, unable to see the racialized and often ugly and violent practices in which it was complicit.

### Slavery

In the seventeenth century, masses of Anglo-Saxon Protestants on what is now American soil bought wholesale into the myth of race as a justification for enslaving African people. Ironically, many Europeans were not wealthy enough to even purchase slaves themselves. In fact, many Europeans in the colonies at that time were themselves indentured servants in no better situation than most Africans initially were. The motivation of wealthy European elites who could actually afford to pay for slaves was obvious; they could increase their production and labor while living more luxurious lives. But what was the motivation for poor Europeans settlers, who wouldn't even be slaveholders themselves, to accept a new racialized and hierarchical order of enslavement?

Part of the reason was simply that, no matter how hard things were, poor whites could count their blessing that they were not black! This offered them a small but important psychological status. That is right: the relative social status of being a part of the newfound "white male citizenry" proved to be more valuable and more important to many people than linking arms with the people who actually had more in common with them economically and socially. The invitation from the elite to participate in the relative psychological gain of white identity and social life outweighed the absolute realities with which these European men were living. The small advantage of white identity blurred the reasoning of these men.

Not everyone quietly accepted this new social order. Enslaved Africans at that same moment were, of course, well situated to call out these changes that qualified and questioned their humanity. It goes without saying, yet must be said anyway: enslaved Africans knew they were more than property, no matter what was said or done to them.

Now, with twenty-first-century hindsight, we can all look back and agree that the white Anglo-Saxons, including Christians, got it terribly wrong. Looking back now, we say that it seems obvious that white people were blinded by their desire for social advantage and superiority. Most American Christians and others would now easily agree with the African perspective of the time and would claim that the African slaves got it right.

### The Dred Scott decision

Let's leap forward a couple of centuries to 1857 and the *Dred Scott* decision at the tail end of the legal chattel slavery era in the United States. Of course our society has always had strange contradictions. Leading up to the late nineteenth century, the United States had been proclaiming universal ideals—such as "all men were created equal"—while simultaneously engaging in some of the cruelest forms of enslavement of African Americans. Dominant cultures have a way of disguising their own oppressive practices from themselves with strong proclamations of innocence and benevolence and universal principles of equality.

Flowing out of that historical context, the supposedly honorable and esteemed Supreme Court of the United States, called to uphold justice and equality, came to the overwhelming conclusion, in a 7–2 decision, that black people were not citizens and would never be. America was never really designed for black people, the justices believed, and therefore black people did not have the right to sue for their freedom when moving into free states. Of course, these men were all products of their time and social location, which many people quickly point out. I agree with those who make that claim, although I am suspicious of why people want to point that out in regard to the slavery era but not for themselves. Being a product of one's time doesn't absolve anyone. We are *all* people of our time. We either renew our minds and become transformed or we conform to the dominant ideologies that convince us that we are moral despite what is going on around us.

After the fact, just about all legal scholars agree that the *Dred Scott* decision was one of the most horrific decisions ever made by the Supreme Court. Unfortunately, at the time it was not obvious to most people who benefited from this arrangement that this was such a terrible decision. At the time, it seemed self-evident to most white people, and it was a boost to the southern way of life and the larger slaveholding economy. This decision had gone through the official legal process, and justice had spoken. White dominant-culture socialization blinded people's moral vision, despite folks like Dred Scott and others who offered a counter perspective.

Dred Scott was also a product of his time. Once again, we can look back and agree that black people at that time correctly understood the problem and that the perspective of the dominant culture was wrong.

### Plessy v. Ferguson

The *Dred Scott* decision was not the only Supreme Court case that we all can look back on and agree was not pleasing to the God revealed in Jesus Christ. Consider *Plessy v. Ferguson* in 1896 as another example. During this 7–1 decision by our highest court, racial segregation was decisively affirmed as legal and as actually promoting of equality.

It is not surprising that most white Americans at that time affirmed the decision. The court merely reflected the popular sentiments of that time. White Christians were also conformed after the same racial patterns of society (or more truthfully, they were the ones laying the foundation for such sentiments). The church took up all sorts of segregated practices during this time, such as black Christians being made second-class citizens in sanctuaries and being confined to balconies and behind ropes. The history of deep racial division in the church that we know all too well flowed out of white Christians affirming racially segregated life as the divine order of things.

Looking back now, most white Americans would agree that the court decision was a terrible one and that white Christians should not have promoted such legalized segregation. While most white Christians reflected the common sentiments of their time, black

Christians continuously and prophetically called out these realities. In that way, white Christians had other Christian voices to which they could have opened themselves up. Most chose not to.

### Civil rights movement

Jump forward to the racial unrest of the mid-twentieth century, which climaxed during the civil rights movement. Most of us have seen the black-and-white footage of black schoolboys and schoolgirls being hosed down against walls and sliding down the street, and of the dogs set loose on them by police during the Birmingham demonstration in 1963. Maybe your mind conjures up the vivid images of Bloody Sunday in Selma, Alabama, where peaceful black marchers, most of them Christians, were violently attacked by state troopers and senselessly beaten. Most American Christians look back at the mid-twentieth century and say that racism was a huge problem. Lynchings of black people were still very prevalent, many black people were prevented from voting, and white supremacist segregation was the law of the land.

Guess what? When polled in May 1946, nearly seven out of ten white Americans surveyed believed that "Negroes in the United States are being treated fairly."[1] Yes, you read that right: in the midst of Jim Crow segregation, the terror of the KKK, the open torment and intimidation by the White Citizens' Council, and the regular violence against black people in America, who had no protection or judicial recourse, most white Americans did not think there was a racial problem. Yes, these numbers included Christians too.

That almost seven out of ten white Americans could think that black people were being treated fairly at such a time of unrest and suffering calls into question the capacity to which any dominant cultural group can discern an oppressive moment with even a little objectivity. Of course, the majority of the black community knew that they were being treated unfairly. In fact, many black Christian leaders were simultaneously attempting to lead the way toward the

1. Rita Simon and Mohamed Alaa Abdel Moneim, *Public Opinion in the United States* (New Brunswick, NJ: Transaction Publishers, 2009), 13; Hazel Gaudet Erskine, "The Polls: Race Relations," *Public Opinion Quarterly* 26, no. 1 (1962), 139.

"beloved community." This vision for a beloved community was the language that Dr. Martin Luther King Jr. frequently employed when prophetically reimagining a new humanity in which racism, classism, and violence would be no more, and where instead there would be mutuality and interdependence.

In contrast, we must seriously wrestle with the fact that so many from the dominant group, in the midst of racial segregation and oppression, could convince themselves that things were already fine and equal for all. This fact is significant background for understanding dominant-group intuitions and assumptions.

## FROM IMPAIRED INTUITION TO SOLIDARITY

What I have tried to do is highlight the dominant culture's failed intuitions throughout the history of the United States. White socialization claimed equality and justice at every stage while also shielding itself from its own oppressive practices and the perspectives of oppressed groups. I want to state an obvious interpretation of this phenomenon in our past and then suggest a Christian practice that recalibrates the witness of the church toward a more faithful trajectory.

First, however, we need to acknowledge that most white Americans (Christians included) have been blind to the racism and oppression that has been so prevalent on this soil for the first 350 years, ever since Jamestown was formed. Most people in the church, whether white or people of color, now agree that from 1619 to the mid-twentieth century, the majority of white Christians, as a part of the dominant group in our society, consistently interpreted things wrongly with regard to racism. The vision of America as a place of justice and equality prevented most people in dominant culture from clearly seeing actual on-the-ground realities. Dominant culture as a social location was actually the *worst* vantage point for deciphering what was going on. It is a given today that dominant society's intuitions were impaired at that time. Almost everyone, except for the very fringe of society, will agree that the majority of white people got it wrong.

As racism mutated in different eras in America, each adaption proved to be just as deceptive for those in the dominant group—not because of their race, but because of their social networks and social location. What we are considering now are the implications of 350 years of misperception by those within dominant society. The dominant group has been unable to recognize, see, or know racial injustice in America because their socialized intuitions shielded them from seeing the concrete realities.

Why does this matter? Well, as I mentioned, polls continually demonstrate that race tends to be a decisive factor in interpreting current, highly charged racial incidents in our country. In many ways, very little has changed in relation to our inability to agree on what is happening in the present. Likewise, I have seen online and in person many people interpret what is going on from the social position of dominant culture. Many white people have quickly dismissed black Americans' experiences of racism in American society. Their own experience and intuition continue to tell them that race is not a significant factor in this country.

Given our history, do we really believe that a people group that benefited from the racial system—socially, economically, politically, or merely psychologically—and whose intuitions were repeatedly wrong for the first 350 years has now suddenly, 400 years in, gained an advantage in interpreting these moments over those whom have been historically oppressed? Even more implausible is that, at this exact moment, the majority of black people who have been right about their own experiences for the past 350 years also instantly, and all at the same time, lost their ability to interpret their own experiences.

Is it likely that the white dominant group and the black marginalized group instantaneously swapped roles regarding who perceives injustice more precisely? Or is it more plausible that dominant culture remains at a limited vantage point for determining what is happening today? To affirm that white people are suddenly getting it right and that black people have simultaneously lost their capacity to interpret their own experiences seems an unhelpful response not based on serious reflection of our past nor the testimonies of African Americans in the present.

The issue before us is the epistemological divide that exists between the dominant group and those living on the underside of the social hierarchy. Those oppressed by dominating and controlling powers tend to hold a different view of the situation than those benefiting from life in a culture and community that violates other people (whether directly or indirectly).

One of the first people to articulate this idea was theologian José Míguez Bonino. He helps us think about how epistemological views are similar to geographical, location-based views. In both cases, one's location (whether social or physical) provides a particular vantage point from which to view an event. Just as with physical location, some social locations offer better vantage points on reality than others. Míguez Bonino asserts, "A social location determines a perspective. It conceals some things and reveals others. We have sometimes referred to this in terms of 'the epistemological privilege of the poor.' The poor are not morally or spiritually superior to others, but they do see reality from a different angle" than those in power do.[2] Therefore, I am suggesting that people on the bottom are better situated to know what is real, and that what they know to be reality is closer to the real thing than the perceptions of those in a dominant social position.

This epistemological advantage, or privileged viewpoint, exists in several ways. First, without the self-interest to remain in denial about social oppression, the proximity of the oppressed to the realities of their own lives puts them at an advantage. Next, most people who are a part of subdominant cultures not only engage deeply with their own viewpoints but also, for survival's sake, must constantly be familiar with the rhetoric, ideologies, and perspectives of the dominant group. This thorough engagement is rarely reciprocated by those in dominant culture, which means that the subdominant group has the advantage of understanding the viewpoints of both sides much more than those on top are able to (an example would be my conversation with my white pastor friend over a cup of sweet tea in which I explained his limited and optional engagement with black community and culture).

Finally, sometimes the very angle from below provides a glance at the ugly underbelly of imperial power, in which the "good face"

2. José Míguez Bonino, *Toward a Christian Political Ethics* (Minneapolis: Fortress Press, 1983), 34.

that it presents to the rest of society is absent. When marginalized people are pushed off ancestral lands and onto reservations, stolen from homelands and enslaved in people's homes, mistreated and othered in their own communities, or told that they will never belong, the dirty secrets of the dominant group are revealed in very vulnerable ways. Subdominant groups need not depend merely on stereotypes created from a distance about "the other" when they are able to share personal stories and experiences within their communities that, when collected, reveal troubling widespread realities. Altogether, the oppressed have an epistemological advantage that allows them to see things more clearly than those whose vision is blocked by denial and distorted by faulty claims of objectivity.

Some people think that because our judicial system has made a verdict on an issue—decisions that are usually in full agreement with dominant cultural norms—justice has spoken and the discussion should be over. This flows out of a naive assumption that our legal system is actually the source that dispenses justice, rather than God.

Black people, however, often know that a verdict and the true reality do not coincide. Jesus' own experience of being arrested at night, put through an unfair trial, and then given a state-sanctioned execution should be the interpretive key for Christians in understanding the inability of empires to dispense true justice. To make my point plain: the judicial system is complicit in the epistemological failures of dominant society. Rarely does the judicial system run counter to the larger and broader mainstream opinions. This doesn't make everything the judicial system does wrong, but it certainly is a far cry from the kind of justice and righteousness that we as Christians are supposed to pursue. Judicial complicity in the dominance of our social hierarchy, especially in light of the system's history, must leave us deeply skeptical about any government's ability to truly let justice roll down like waters.

What we are moving toward as a solution is completely counterintuitive. Those on the margins or in the cracks of society often found themselves intimately sharing life with God in the form of Jesus Christ, who chose to especially identify himself with such rejected people. Jesus did so to the point that he himself became "the stone the builders rejected" (Psalm 118:22 NIV). In 1 John 2:6 we are reminded of the New Testament challenge to follow after Jesus—as his disciples, to "walk just as Jesus walked." In following Jesus' footsteps, we have a new pattern that can help us break out of the cycle which leads to blinders around racism and to faulty intuitions. Those in dominant culture are now freed to commune with oppressed people and to learn from them how to see a truer social reality, one closer to the vantage point of our crucified Christ. The challenge here is to trust the intuition of oppressed people over against one's own gut and experience, which has proven to lead dominant groups astray.

White American Christians in our society must do something seemingly absurd and unnatural, yet very Christian in orientation: they must move decisively toward a counterintuitive solidarity with those on the margins. They must allow the eyes of the violated of the land to lead and guide them, seeking to have renewed minds no longer conformed to the patterns of our world. *poor people march*

## BONHOEFFER'S HARLEM EXPERIENCES

On February 4, 1906, Dietrich Bonhoeffer was born to an elite, upper-class, and well-connected German family. To his father's surprise (and probably horror), Dietrich decided to pursue a profession doing theology. Bonhoeffer's understanding at this early time seems to be exclusively informed by a highly sacramental Lutheran theology. Add to that his highly nationalistic orientation, which uncritically combined German identity with Christianity, and it becomes clear that Bonhoeffer began as a theologian well poised to bolster and uphold the soon-to-come Third Reich. In his early years, he even evoked Constantine's legacy, assuring his people that in the symbol of the cross, "only in this sign will you be victorious!" During one lecture series, Bonhoeffer argued for setting aside Jesus' Sermon on the Mount as something to live by, and suggested that loving enemies in an actual national conflict is impossible. His life experience as a social elite, with a theology informed by an unexamined nationalistic and dominant cultural ideology, had Bonhoeffer on a trajectory of becoming a well-respected theologian in both the pre-Nazi context and the Nazi era that was just around the corner.

The Christian journey can easily move from cheap grace to costly grace, however, because all things are possible with God. That certainly was the case for Bonhoeffer. After he traveled the world and finished up his dissertation, *Sanctorum Communio*, in Berlin in 1927, Bonhoeffer decided to put off concluding his postdoctoral work so that he could travel and learn more. In the 1930–31 academic year he found himself once again in the class-room, but now in New York City, studying at Union Theological Seminary. As a German-trained theologian, he initially scoffed at the political orientation of the praxis-focused Union students, who in his mind didn't really know how to do real theology. But while he was at Union, Bonhoeffer made several important friendships that would change him. Those friendships would increase his own capacity to perceive our troubled society as a disciple of Jesus for the rest of his life.

One of those friends was Jean Lasserre, a student from France. Despite the obstacles that French and German students would have had at the time, because of the conflicts between their homelands, Lasserre and Bonhoeffer made it work. Lasserre introduced Bon-hoeffer to a pacifist Christian perspective shaped by the Sermon on the Mount, and this quickly began to challenge Bonhoeffer dramatically on many fronts. The life, teachings, death, and resur-rection of Christ would become central and ongoing frameworks for Bonhoeffer going forward. This turn toward the Sermon on the Mount meant that discipleship and formation in the way of Jesus would become central themes for Bonhoeffer, especially in his final days and writings.

It was Franklin Fisher, however, a Negro student from Ala-bama, who provided Bonhoeffer with an invaluable gift. Though Bonhoeffer was generally disappointed by American churches, his ecclesial and Christological questions were about to get flipped upside down. Fisher was one of the few black students at Union Seminary at the time, and he would later have direct involvement in the civil rights movement, alongside Martin Luther King Jr. At this time, however, Fisher was an intern at Abyssinian Baptist Church in Harlem. This was and still is a famous black congregation. At that time it was being pastored by Adam Clayton Powell Sr., and was known for its social and political engagement and for being a beacon of justice during an extremely troubled time in the African American community. The challenges of the early twentieth century called for bold and courageous faith that took visible action in the community.

This community would prove to be liberating for Bonhoeffer. Fisher invited Bonhoeffer to break a taboo by crossing racial boundaries of belonging, not only into the black Harlem community, but also within the black church. And it was here, among a marginalized group trying to survive the struggles of white supremacy, white terrorism, and the Great Depression, that Bonhoeffer met the Jesus who stood in solidarity with oppressed and suffering people. This was a life-changing, reorienting encounter with Jesus and with the black community that worshiped and followed him.

As the pastor, Adam Clayton Powell Sr. was not afraid to preach Jesus and his kingdom of justice. Bonhoeffer was captivated by the "black Christ" and the vehicle of black preaching that introduced him to Jesus anew. Bonhoeffer began purchasing albums of Negro spirituals, as he was drawn to their piety and spiritual depth. He would later share them with his students back in Germany. Bonhoeffer began reading black intellectuals like W. E. B. DuBois and Harlem Renaissance thinkers, who stretched his social imagination. Bonhoeffer became a lay teacher for Sunday school kids in the church. He traveled to Howard College (now Howard University) to meet some of the gifted black intellectuals he had read and studied. Seeing the racialized criminal system at work, Bonhoeffer wrote to friends in Europe to advocate against the Scottsboro trials and the terrible racial injustices that America permitted to occur. He even once experienced being denied service at a restaurant with a black friend. These experiences and others helped reorient Bonhoeffer's whole faith toward following Jesus, obeying the Sermon on the Mount, and living in solidarity and relationship with this oppressed black community. Harlem and this black church gave him new eyes.

Unfortunately, most people are not familiar with this period in Bonhoeffer's life. American dominant culture is primarily obsessed with his participation in the resistance of Hitler's regime in 1933 and onward until his death. What gets lost is that Bonhoeffer was able to speak and see the injustice and evil of the Third Reich in a way that most of his German theological colleagues could not at that time. Most of them were still rooted in the same nationalistic entanglements with Christianity with which Bonhoeffer began. They could not see the racial problem in its depth. They had been socialized, largely through a distorted Christianity, to *not* perceive the depth of the problem until it was too late. Bonhoeffer had learned to see Jesus anew and to understand what was going on in his society by following Christ into solidarity with the oppressed, whether black Christians in America or Jews in Germany. This counterintuitive solidarity gave him new eyes to see and evaluate the world.

Bonhoeffer stumbled upon a counterintuitive Christian solidarity and faith, an intimate experience of placing his body among those on the underside of the racialized hierarchy. He would continue to wrestle with Christological questions, understanding more and more the significance of Jesus who suffered and rose again, but all from the vantage point of those systemically marginalized in society. His commitments to accept the costs of discipleship would ultimately end his life, as he was arrested and then later hung in a concentration camp.

Bonhoeffer wrote a powerful letter to his inner circle of trusted friends and family right before his arrest and eventual state execution in a concentration camp. In the letter, we can get a sense of the transformation that he continued to go through, up until the very end. His transformation is one the whole church must go through if we are going to be faithful in responding to the racialized hierarchy that we have created, permitted, accommodated, or consented to for so long. Bonhoeffer wrote:

It remains an experience of incomparable value that we have for once learned to see the great events of world history from below, from the perspective of the outcasts, the suspects, the maltreated, the powerless, the oppressed and reviled, in short from the perspective of the suffering. If only during this time bitterness and envy have not corroded the heart; that we come to see matters great and small, happiness and misfortune, strength and weakness with new eyes; that our sense for greatness, humanness, justice, and mercy has grown clearer, freer, more incorruptible; that we learn, indeed, that personal suffering is a more useful key, a more fruitful principle than personal happiness for exploring the meaning of the world in contemplation and action.[3]

## DR. KING'S LIFELONG JOURNEY

On January 15, 1929, Martin Luther King Jr. was born. Actually, he was initially named Michael, and continued to be called Mike by many close friends and family. King was also born into relative wealth, at least in relation to most black people at the time. In Atlanta, King was raised in a neighborhood called "Sweet Auburn," a stable, middle-class, African American community filled mostly with black professionals. King's family found themselves part of this middle-class neighborhood because his father was a pastor, which would have certainly been one of the most stable and reliable vocations for a black person at that time. Martin Luther King Jr. entered Morehouse College at the young age of fifteen.

Receiving these social and economic advantages exposed King to so much more than he would have otherwise. It expanded his horizons and stretched his social and theological frameworks. Coming from a line of preachers, King also had a pastoral vocation in his sights. Rather than stay in the South, he headed up north for graduate school. His northern education included Crozer Theological Seminary in Pennsylvania and a PhD program at Boston University. Understanding King's life and significance must begin with recognizing the complexity of his life as a black man who had advantages that most black people in the twentieth century could not access. In 1954 King and his wife, Coretta, moved to

3. Dietrich Bonhoeffer, *Letters and Papers from Prison*, Dietrich Bonhoeffer Works, vol. 8 (Minneapolis: Fortress Press, 2010), 52.

Montgomery, Alabama, where he began to pastor Dexter Avenue Baptist Church. He was only twenty-five years old when he took on the responsibility of pastoring this middle- and upper-class black community. Initially King had no intention of leading any civil rights movements, and instead was focused on finishing his dissertation, growing church membership, and establishing himself as a pastor.

This deeply segregated city was thrown into the national scene one year later when Rosa Parks, an activist and secretary for the local chapter of the NAACP, courageously challenged the humiliating, racialized bus seating in Montgomery. She refused to get up and give her seat to a white man on her ride home. This public action was supported by the local black clergy, and then by the broader African American community. The Montgomery Improvement Association, created to support Parks's action, appointed a young and talented new minister, Martin Luther King Jr., as its president and spokesperson. King initially did not accept the invitation. Eventually he did, however, and this position would soon have him front and center in the public square.

King's hesitancy is important to note. His goal as a pastor had been relative comfort, especially if he could keep his head down and not attract too much attention from the white establishment in the South. King's decision to be a spokesperson for the movement, however, resulted in almost immediate trouble for him and his family. He began receiving death threats, crosses were burned in his yard, and bricks were thrown through his front window. Merely mimicking the faith of his parents would no longer suffice, not through this storm. King would have to move from theory and propositions in his head to an active faith in God that would carry him through.

This happened for him after an anonymous midnight call, only two months into the Montgomery Bus Boycott. The caller said, "Listen, nigger, we've taken all we want from you; before next week you'll be sorry you ever came to Montgomery."[4] This shook King, and he was on the verge of giving up. Then, in what would

4. Martin Luther King Jr., *Stride toward Freedom: The Montgomery Story* (Boston: Beacon Press, 2010), 124.

be a critical moment in his life, King had a profound encounter
with God in his kitchen over a cup of coffee. King later recounted:

> With my cup of coffee sitting untouched before me I tried to
> think of a way to move out of the picture without appearing
> a coward. In this state of exhaustion, when my courage had
> all but gone, I decided to take my problem to God. With
> my head in my hands, I bowed over the kitchen table and
> prayed aloud. The words I spoke to God that midnight are
> still vivid in my memory. "I am here taking a stand for what
> I believe is right. But now I am afraid. The people are look-
> ing to me for leadership, and if I stand before them without
> strength and courage, they too will falter. I am at the end
> of my powers. I have nothing left. I've come to the point
> where I can't face it alone." At that moment I experienced
> the presence of the Divine as I had never experienced Him
> before. It seemed as though I could hear the quiet assurance
> of an inner voice saying: "Stand up for righteousness, stand
> up for truth; and God will be at your side forever." Almost
> at once my fears began to go. My uncertainty disappeared. I
> was ready to face anything.[5]

It took a year of boycotts, but eventually the buses were deseg-
regated. Beginning in the 1960s, King would become increasingly
inspired by the young people involved in the Student Nonviolent
Coordinating Committee, who radicalized nonviolent resistance
and protest by putting their very bodies on the line through sit-ins,
freedom rides, and other creative protests to accomplish their goals.
With such inspiration, in 1963, King and his organizational team,
the Southern Christian Leadership Conference (SCLC), imple-
mented "Project C," which was designed to create citywide "confrontation" and disruption in Birmingham, Alabama. Birmingham
was such a violent and racist city, with so many bombings and
other incidents of violence committed against black communities
and churches, that its nickname was "Bombingham." King and
the SCLC moved away from simply attacking segregation to putting economic pressure on the city. That success, followed by the

5. Ibid., 125.

1965 protests in Selma, Alabama, which focused on protecting
the voting rights of African Americans, points toward King's ever-
increasing analysis of the problems that America faced. In 1963
King might have spoken about "a dream," but his optimism was
turning into a more truthful assessment of our racialized and hierarchical society. His perceptions were now shaped by his grassroots activity on the ground.

After securing voting rights legislation in 1965, the SCLC
immediately turned its attention to northern cities, particularly
Chicago. These cities represented the complexity of our racialized and classed society because they were not benefiting from the
desegregation of businesses and schools in the South. So in January 1966, King and his family moved into a slum apartment on
the south side of Chicago. His decision to move into the neighborhood, and to live in solidarity with oppressed black people in the
North, demonstrated how far he had come from "Sweet Auburn"
and his early goals of merely living a quiet and comfortable life
as a pastor in the South. He was now ready to struggle with these
residents against sophisticated racialized systems and economic
pressures that were crushing them daily. He found that address-
ing the northern housing patterns was much more difficult than
desegregating the South.

His failures in the North could point to the fact that the "Chicago Plan" worked too well. For example, when he and others
demonstrated in Gage Park, an exclusively white community, they
were met with all the hatred and violence that they had come to
expect in the South—and much worse. Cars were burned, guns
were fired, and King was struck in the head by a brick. Watching
the video footage of King during this time, you can see the deep
fear he had as he walked through this community in the North and
realized he could die at any moment. This was in the late 1960s,
more than ten years after the Montgomery demonstrations. The
only difference between the South and the North, he discovered,
was that he hadn't earned any sympathy from white America for
his actions in the North like he had in the South.

King's tone and vision would continue to morph and adjust as
he made sense of northern injustice, racism, and white apathy. He

began to connect the dots of white supremacy and violence around the globe to the black experience in the United States. He courageously began speaking out against the Vietnam War, delivering one of his most radical messages ever, entitled "Beyond Vietnam," at Riverside Church in 1967. King began naming the "Giant Triplets"—racism, materialism, and militarism. These three issues, he believed, were intertwined and central influences over American life.

The late 1960s also birthed a powerful black consciousness movement. King began to understand how much antiblack ideology and sentiments had shaped black self-identities and psyches. Speaking to a crowd, he declared, "Somebody told a lie one day. They couched it in language. They made everything Black ugly and evil. Look in your dictionaries and see the synonyms of the word Black. It's always something degrading and low and sinister. Look at the word White, it's always something pure, high and clean. Well I want to get the language right tonight." And therefore King encouraged the crowd to affirm their humanity to themselves: "I'm Black and I'm beautiful!"[6]

In early 1968, King began unrolling the Poor People's Campaign, which was a devastating condemnation of American economic life. By tackling poverty, King desired to bring economically oppressed people together into solidarity, whether they were black, Native American, Hispanic, Asian, or white. With consideration of the overlaps of race and class, King decided to turn his attention to the protests unfolding in Memphis. He deeply desired to be present and in bodily agreement with black sanitation workers who were seeking equal pay and safer working conditions. It was a spontaneous trip, and some of his colleagues advised against it, but King felt he needed to stand with these poor black workers.

Unfortunately, white supremacist hate caught up to Martin Luther King Jr. in Memphis. He was assassinated on April 4, 1968, because of his firm solidarity with the oppressed. Beyond his famous "I Have a Dream" speech in 1963, we find a disciple,

6. "Dr. Martin Luther King Jr.: 'I'm Black and I'm Beautiful' [VIDEO]," NewsOne video, January 20, 2014, http://newsone.com/2843703/dr-martin-l-king-jr-im-black -and-im-beautiful-video/.

preacher, and activist. He certainly stumbled and failed along the way, yet he persisted in trying to understand and challenge the hierarchies and systemic violence that shaped everyday life for millions of people. For King, Jesus led into a counterintuitive path from relative comfort and job security to true solidarity with the oppressed of the land. From that vantage point, he continually grew throughout his life to see things as they truly were and to know how Jesus provided another way of life.

This call to *not* go with your gut—to move toward an intimate, transformative, and relational solidarity with marginalized and oppressed people—is not easy. It requires learning to see again, from oppressed people's perception of things, rather than through one's own lens. However, I believe that Jesus' own emptying of himself and taking on the form of a slave models for us the way forward (Philippians 2:5-8). We are called to imitate the same Jesus who is alive and still leading his followers alongside the oppressed of our day.

Discipleship is the cure for dominant cultural blinders that leave people's intuition and vision impaired and unreliable. *Not* going with your gut, when it is socialized by dominant culture, and moving toward counterintuitive solidarity with the oppressed, must be understood as a Christian discipline, as necessary a practice for Christian formation as is praying, gathering in Christian community, reading Scripture, sharing resources, worshiping, and giving thanks. The Spirit of Jesus Christ is drawing all of us to see things "from below."

# 5

# WHITENESS MATTERS

**N**o matter where I have lived, I have eventually had to come to terms with the reality that racial hierarchy is always present, and that whiteness, without fail, matters.

After graduating from college, I was immediately hired to be the pastor over the youth ministries at Harrisburg Brethren in Christ Church in Harrisburg, Pennsylvania. This is an urban Anabaptist community pursuing racial reconciliation and holistic ministry in the neighborhood.[1] It is not a perfect community, but it is striving after Jesus. I learned a lot during my time there, from both the highs and lows of church ministry and community life. While I was there, I was at the forefront of engaging racialized obstacles that prevented us from embodying our own vision to become the new humanity in Christ. In many ways, it was the perfect place for me to find my own voice, gifts, and passions.

Living in Harrisburg also provided a great space for reflection for me. It is the capital of Pennsylvania, but it is much smaller than

1. Contemporary Anabaptism grew out of the sixteenth-century Anabaptist movement that emerged as the radical wing of the Protestant Reformation. Anabaptists insisted on centralizing discipleship to Jesus, breaking the church from top-down state power, and creating voluntary communities of mutual aid that renounced violence, among other things. The theology, practice, and customs of Anabaptist Christian communities today are inspired by this Jesus-shaped movement of radical reformation, seeking to keep it a living tradition for the contemporary context.

Philadelphia. Its size makes the racial divisions in the area more visible. On any given day, you might find yourself frequently and quickly crossing back and forth into different racialized spaces. Uptown Harrisburg is a historic black neighborhood. Midtown and downtown are mostly white and often well-off. And then there is Allison Hill, which is where I lived. It is a diverse, socioeconomically challenged section of the city. Though mostly black and Hispanic, Allison Hill also has residents from other racial and ethnic groups.

Living in Harrisburg was a time for healing and affirmation of my personhood and psyche after three years of living in a white suburb outside of Philadelphia followed by four years as a minority on a mostly white, Christian college campus. On my block on Chestnut Street, I felt at home. I felt like I belonged. And I began feeling a bit more like a "regular person" again, like I had once felt growing up in Norristown: not constantly consumed with how my body was being differentiated and interpreted by others around me. The surrounding blocks where I lived were primarily African American, and it became an important space for me to consider and more deeply reflect on what it means to be black in America.

## HARRISBURG INVASION DAY

On one occasion I remember leaving my house and hopping into my '92 Mercury Sable on a short commute to another part of the city. I began driving down Market Street, a major road in this part of town. As I headed toward downtown through Allison Hill, something quickly caught my attention. On my left up ahead, I saw a large mass of people. Tons of white people had gathered together in a large bunch on the sidewalk.

This was a bit odd. You don't normally see a lot of white people in this part of town. So of course my curiosity was piqued. The first thing I observed as I approached was that they were all wearing bright, loud, matching yellow T-shirts. They clearly didn't want to be missed. White people were here!

I was still confused about what, exactly, was going on. Was a large white youth group doing a week of service, possibly doing repairs on homes? As I got closer, I realized that that wasn't the case. They had a large stash of grocery bags, and they were randomly passing them out to everyone who walked by. It was like an old episode of *The Oprah Winfrey Show*, in which everyone in the studio suddenly became a winner. If you happened to be walking down the street at this moment, guess what—you got groceries!

Now let me be honest: I am not impressed with this sort of drive-by approach to service. There are much more strategic ways to get food to the people who need it than to randomly hand it out to every person walking down the sidewalk. When you just plop yourself in another community without any local guidance, this is what happens.

At first I didn't really care that much. I just thought to myself, "Silly church folk," and shook my head. But everything changed for me as I drove parallel to the little show being put on. I was now close enough to read the words on their T-shirts. The words printed front and center on those bright T-shirts were "Harrisburg Invasion Day."

Later I talked to some other Harrisburg residents about what I had seen. Apparently some mostly white churches from outside Allison Hill had collaborated to pull this off. Each year they worked together to plan and coordinate the "invasion" of our black and brown neighborhood for Jesus by handing out groceries to random people and holding a block party. They would quickly move in, do their good deeds, and then vanish just as quickly as they had first appeared.

I don't imagine that they understood how condescending and paternalistic their actions looked, and I am hopeful that this has stopped by now. Yet we must take seriously these questions: What caused them to think that they ought to invade another community's space in such a way? Why did they come without working with the already existing black and brown groups and leaders who have been engaging in creative and restorative ministry in the city? Were we, in their eyes, so helpless and needy that they thought the only imaginable solution was to coordinate a one-day drive-through "invasion" of our pathetic and pathological community? Why didn't they see those of us engaged in this work as a resource, as teachers to learn from? Why did they establish themselves as the hosts and saviors of our community? Did they not see the residents of our community as having worth, able to offer them something that they needed as well?

This group was performing something very particular—what we could call "white Christian social practice." It is precisely *my* need to add "white" before "Christian social practice" that must be investigated. I am sure that even calling a certain kind of social practice "white" will bother some people. Often when race is talked about in dominant cultural spaces, everything gets named except whiteness. Black and brown descriptions are used all the time. People have no problem describing a black person's race in casual conversation. It matters what is said and what is not said. Race always means something in our language, even if we are unconscious of what we are implying.

Ironically, dominant society will proclaim colorblindness at one moment and then the next moment will have no problem calling out "black-on-black violence" instead of just seeing it as human-on-human violence. When something is believed to be problematic in African American communities, colorblind rhetoric disappears, and blackness is quickly named without reserve. I have never heard anyone talk about the problem of "white-on-white violence" even though, according to statistics, this type of violence occurs at very similar rates as that of black-on-black violence.

What is important for us to consider now, however, is this: What precisely does it mean to be white in our society? What is whiteness, and what is its socially constructed function in society? In the church we must learn to change our view of racism in society as merely a "black issue." Instead, we must look at the other end of the racial hierarchy to explore those who have been operating out of superiority, dominance, and control as a collective in the United States. In this chapter I suggest that whiteness matters.

## WHAT DOES IT MEAN TO BE WHITE?

So what does it mean to be white? Saying that someone is white is saying more than just that someone is of European descent and heritage, though that is normally all we mean when we use the term. There is a gap between how we use the term *white* and the way that whiteness functions on people's behalf in society. *White* is the pseudoscientific and socially constructed category used to centralize power among a certain portion of humanity and at the direct harm and cost of people of color, especially Native American and black life in America. And it is not a static category. Whiteness subtly shifts and changes over time as necessary.

To be white is not only to be Euro-American; it is also to identify with, and participate in, the life of a sociopolitical collective that created this artificially constructed racial identity to accomplish something. People move from identifying with a particular European people group—for example, the Irish—to identifying as a white person for a reason. This is a decision European immigrants made over and over again in America, such that the definition of and borders around who was white continuously expanded. In the seventeenth century, only Anglo-Saxon Protestants were considered white, but the definition eventually grew to include Irish Catholics, Italians, and other groups who were initially excluded. This was politically strategic. It formed a large enough collective power in society that continuously reproduced a system of advantage for whites at the direct expense of people of color. At the very minimum, being white has meant benefiting from and obtaining an ongoing preference and advantage in a nation and economy built on the stolen land of Native Americans and the stolen labor of African Americans. Being white usually means never having to think about it that way during one's day-to-day life.

America is a thoroughly racialized society dominated and controlled by white people in a manner that advantages them because of their whiteness. Even poor whites, who are economically deprived, will find at critical moments that, all things being equal, being white is more socially advantageous than being black. And many people don't realize just how socially constructed a white identity is, and how it has been conveniently changed over and over again to let some people in and to exclude others. What defined a white person several centuries ago is not what we mean by it now. It conveniently mutates according to the political whims of the dominant society of each generation.

It is important to remember that there is no authentic, biological substance to the idea of race.[2] Europeans constructed black and white categories for a reason. Whiteness mattered because it provided economic, social, and political benefits. For example, immigrants in the early twentieth century understood very well what white status meant if obtained, and therefore they went to court arguing to be recognized under the law as such. As the authors of *The Color of Wealth* write:

> Court decisions on white status were based on a mix of supposedly scientific criteria and the common understandings of the day, leading to a mess of contradictions. Syrians were deemed white in 1909, 1910, and 1915, but not in 1913 or 1914. Asian Indians won white status in 1910, 1913, 1919, and 1920, but not in 1909, 1917, or after 1923. The persistence of immigrants in suing for whiteness is evidence of the financial and social benefits that came with white status. After all, no one sued to be considered Asian, much less black.[3]

Even today, I'm pretty sure when people get pulled over by a cop, they are not thinking, "Well geez, I really wish I could put on black skin right now; that would really work to my favor!" People can talk all they want about reverse racism, but when the rubber hits the road, most people know deep down that racial profiling, in all its different manifestations, would disadvantage them if they were black. In the dominant culture of America, blackness has been the antithesis of whiteness, its polarizing opposite. It has been placed at the far bottom of the social hierarchy that, consciously or unconsciously, places whiteness at the top.

Whiteness matters when it advantages those seen as having pure European ancestry. Whether you are considering government leadership, the heads of corporations, or even Christian organizations, it becomes clear that white people are disproportionately represented across the board. They often get their positions because they know someone—a friend, church member, or relative—who

2. Michael Omi and Howard Winant, *Racial Formation in the United States*, 3rd ed. (New York: Routledge, 2014), 115–20.
3. Meizhu Lui et al., *The Color of Wealth: The Story Behind the U.S. Racial Wealth Divide* (New York: New Press, 2006), 250.

is positioned to help them and not necessarily because they are the most qualified person for the job. Whiteness can't promise a good life, but it does provide a social system that operates to most Euro-American persons' advantage.

Many people are unaware of the various white advantages that have been offered legally in our country, falsely thinking that slavery was the only significant differentiation. In reality, things like redlining, housing discrimination, and other historic racialized practices offered great advantages, socially and economically, to white households. Just one example is the Homestead Act of 1862, which "gave millions of acres to white settlers. . . . Overall, 1.5 million families got ownership of 246 million acres of land from the various homestead programs, nearly as much land as California and Texas combined. One study estimates the number of Americans living today who are descendants of homestead recipients at forty-six million."[4]

What people do not understand is that African Americans were simultaneously being denied access to these large wealth-accumulating programs. The authors of *The Color of Wealth* note that an 1826 law prevented African Americans from preemption rights, and that in 1857 the U.S. Land Office denied public land grants to African Americans.[5]

Millions of white families have benefited from the Homestead Act or even the GI Bill, both of which were often denied to African Americans who migrated all over the country for better opportunities in America. White Americans have benefited from some of the largest government handouts in history (beyond, of course, the stolen land and stolen labor). And even for those who have not directly received any of those white benefits, just being white meant access to live in, do business with, and benefit from communities that had created their wealth through such racially stratified and oppressive practices and policies. My brief account doesn't even scratch the surface of the ways that the white dominant group has received concrete social, political, and economic benefits from racial oppression.

---

4. Ibid., 241.
5. Ibid.

## DISADVANTAGE, OVER-ADVANTAGE

In American society we commonly talk about "disadvantaged communities." What is odd is that we rarely explore the implications of the existence of disadvantaged groups in relation to what it means to be white in America.

If there are systemically disadvantaged people, then there must be *over*-advantaged people. How often do we talk about particular people and communities as "over-advantaged"? We feel free to talk about how someone is from a "disadvantaged" neighborhood or school, but we do it as though that community lives in a social vacuum. It is as though someone just happens to be structurally disadvantaged.

Talking about whiteness can seem a bit innocuous, because we usually don't talk about it in terms of the apparent systemic social advantage and hierarchy. And even if we were to talk about such realities, we are nonetheless taught to get all the advantages and privileges we can grab hold of in America. We can begin an honest assessment of the situation only when we acknowledge this fact: the systemic advantages from which you unconsciously benefit are simultaneously harmful to someone else.

Let's consider how a system of advantaging whiteness harms the well-being of black people. In a University of Chicago study, resumes were sent to employers in response to employment ads in the newspaper. The resumes were fictitious ones created for the study. The researchers sought to measure racial bias by sending out some resumes with names traditionally associated with black Americans and other resumes with names traditionally associated with white Americans.

The researchers found that fictitious job applicants with common "white" names needed to send out ten resumes to get a call back, while applicants with traditional "black" names needed to send out fifteen to get a call back. It is important to understand that this was done with all qualifications in the resumes being equal. Also realize that employers had not even seen the applicants face-to-face. Advantages and disadvantages are distributed according to racial categories before someone even walks into the room.[6]

Along the same lines, another study explored the impact of race and criminal records on employment opportunities. The researchers focused on the earliest stages of the employment process (so again, there are even more opportunities for race to play a role later on as well). Researchers had male study participants go to various businesses and fill out applications. The goal was to see who either got an interview on the spot or later received a callback, both of which were considered to be positive responses.

Researchers chose a pair of white men and a pair of black men to play the roles of ex-offender applicants and applicants without any criminal convictions. They found that the white men without a criminal conviction had a 34 percent positive response. White men with a conviction, however, only had a 17 percent positive response. We can see from this that criminal convictions hold a deep stigma in our society, cutting white men's positive response percentage in half because they had to "check the box."

But the most alarming result was the black men's positive response percentage, particularly for those without a conviction. Black men *without* a conviction only had a 14 percent positive response. This means that white men *with* a conviction have more positive employment responses than black men *without* a conviction.

Let that sink in for a moment.

Finally, black men with a conviction only had a 5 percent positive response in the initial stage of the employment process. Blackness and criminality, when combined, create social death for many people.[7]

This type of study (of which there are many, with each study individually only scratching the surface of the issue) easily reveals

6. Marianne Bertrand and Sendhil Mullainathan, "Are Emily and Greg More Employable than Lakisha and Jamal? A Field Experiment on Labor Market Discrimination" (working paper no. 9873, National Bureau of Economic Research, Cambridge, MA, 2003).

7. Devah Pager, "The Mark of a Criminal Record" (Center for Demography and Ecology, University of Madison–Wisconsin, 2002).

the significance of a racialized system of advantage and disadvantage. Whiteness matters. The manner in which black men in the employment process are being discriminated against—not to mention other racial minorities and women—directly benefits white men, because now they have a greater chance at getting a job because of the lack of opportunity experienced by racial minorities. And yet dominant culture never talks about American society as a racialized state that is dominated and controlled by white people and that advantages whiteness, often through subtle and possibly unconscious bias. Clearly this preference for white men in the employment process is just one more example of how whiteness matters in our society.

## THE DILEMMA OF NICE WHITE PEOPLE

These realities are often hard to accept. For white people to acknowledge these social advantages in regard to their families, friends, coworkers, church members, and themselves is difficult. The stumbling block for many people is the conviction that their social networks couldn't *possibly* be racially prejudiced because they are full of such nice people. How could such nice people be racists?

I struggled through this question when I was wrestling with racism on my Christian college campus. It was one of the friendliest places I had ever been. It could almost at times seem unreal, with all the waving and smiling going on around me. These cultural manners seemed odd to me at first. Yet this was the same space in which I experienced the most severe and hostile racism. Strangely, in this nicest of places I was repeatedly treated like a thug or a threat. I found myself foolishly trying to prove my humanity over and over again to each new group of white people I encountered. What a draining experience that was!

So why did so many nice, friendly white people, whose stereotypes of black men I had eventually broken, continue to gaze at other black bodies with that same distorted vision? For many of my white peers, interaction with any one black person didn't necessarily challenge their stereotypes. Instead, they seemed to have a preset way of making sense of each individual black person's unique and distinct personality. I believe this was done by catego-rizing those in their relational networks as an exception to their rule. Rather than breaking the racist rule altogether, many white people view any particular black person they come to know as an exception to the rule. This means that, for many white people, black people in general are still lazy, less smart, threatening, and immoral—even as they perceive that there are exceptional black people they know personally who don't fit that description. And these aren't the mean and nasty folks we are talking about; these are often extremely nice white people.

I learned some important lessons about how white people themselves are often perceived by others during my seven years of living predominantly within white cultural spaces (three years in high school and four years in college). In high school I learned that young white kids who smoked weed or did much more serious drugs were not considered to be a threat to the fabric of society, as black youth who do drugs are. Instead, the white kids were seen as "experimenting"—you know, "just being kids." These habits didn't stigmatize their humanity. They could still be considered generally good kids of societal worth even while everyone knew that they were regular marijuana smokers. Dominant culture val-ued their humanity no matter what they got into. Despite the high levels of drug use I saw happening around me, there was no war on drugs going on. No white suburban neighborhoods were being put under surveillance, and no white kids were being stopped and frisked on their walk home. And there certainly were very few arrests (I can't remember any white teens being arrested for drugs even once during my time at this mostly white, middle-class school). Regardless, it was clear that the culture interpreted white teen bodies as basically innocent and harmless, except for the most severe and extreme situations.

My time living on a Christian college campus allowed me to see deeper within the logic of whiteness. I saw how a culture of niceness could be combined with the dangerous ideologies that are death-dealing to communities of color. In particular, the unre-lenting white gaze on black bodies, although leveled by friendly people, unveiled for me the ways that blackness meant, for many, guilty until proven innocent. It was a culture in which racial minorities frequently had to prove themselves worthy of respect.

Again, when I talk to white Christians, many seem to have trouble believing that someone from their neighborhood, church, school, family, or social network could have antiblack racist perceptions. The folks in their networks are all just so *nice*. Somehow, American society has allowed the idea to prevail that it takes mean people to perpetuate white supremacy. We have bought into the idea that our friendliness is evidence that we couldn't have adopted subtle antiblack ideologies so common in dominant culture. For too long, too many have assumed that nice white people couldn't be complicit with a white-controlled and white-dominated society, because they are so fun to be around.

But the truth is that white racism doesn't exist only in the KKK bogeyman of the past. Instead, it is pervasive within the air of dominant culture in subtle, nuanced, and often unconscious ways. To acknowledge this doesn't mean that your network is full of mean people. I don't question the fact that many white people are extremely nice, but I still believe that most are socialized by and participate in a white dominant culture that has become adjusted to white supremacy and racial marginalization.

White racism has always been veiled by "civil" culture. The first necessity is to interpret society's way of life with high ideals. More than just nice, it is civil, fair, equal, and just. In our day, the colorblind rhetoric is a mutated form of this approach. Notice that it is primarily white conservative Americans, and decisively not African Americans, who praise colorblindness as our path toward a better future. Dominant culture has an advantage in disseminating its ideas and claims, and it has done a masterful job at defining how it wants to be interpreted.

One of the central concepts around race, communicated over and over again by dominant culture, is that we ought to be colorblind and that talking about race has no place in our society. But two hands work collaboratively in our white supremacist culture, and the "colorblind" hand is just one of them. The other hand of a white supremacist culture deals out highly racialized practices. This is ideological work being done behind its own back. It's like those who lie so much and so pathologically that they are able to convince themselves of their own lies. That is how American dominant culture frequently works. American life is saturated in racial practices and sentiments. Most white people live extremely racialized and segregated lives, even when they live in diverse neighborhoods (though that itself is rare). And our society is so permeated with racism that we can actually predict many people's life experiences and opportunities based on their race.

The depth of our racialized society is beyond most of our comprehension. And this is precisely because the first hand has done such a powerful job in normalizing our racialized lives. White supremacy thrives off unexamined claims of colorblindness while simultaneously engaging in highly racialized practices.

## WESTERN FIRST, CHRISTIAN SECOND

One of the challenges we now face is that the culture and norms of the white dominant group are always presumed to be right and moral, and not in need of patient and careful investigation. This is evident wherever Western European colonizers and missionaries have imposed their culture and values through mission and church life. Today, you could go to every continent on the earth on any given Sunday and find Western-style church buildings with organs and pianos on opposing sides of the pulpit and with pictures of white Jesus prominently positioned. The pastors and most of the church members will likely be wearing nonindigenous clothes, their Western best: suit and tie or dress. Familiar melodies of Western hymns will play a significant role. And oddly, many of the Christian people of the town will bear Western names. Why do they do all this? Well, it is because they have been given the gospel of Jesus Christ, right?

Well, not quite. The missionaries came promising Jesus. But Christianity was so entangled in Western culture that the missionaries imposed Western civilization on people in the name of Jesus rather than vulnerably bearing witness to the life, teachings, death, and resurrection of Jesus in word and deed and then letting the Holy Spirit do its work. It seems that it was not Jesus' body at the center of Western Christian life and imagination. Instead, as Willie James Jennings has put it, "The body of another has remained at the center of our relational imagination, the body of a powerful, white, Western man, the image of self-sufficiency, social power, and self-determination."[8] Missionaries often tried to make indigenous people become Western first, Christian second.

If you think that this claim is a bit much, we must ask, whose body were people being converted after? Into whose likeness were they being formed? Upon conversion, indigenous people often had to get Western haircuts, wear Western clothes, learn Western languages, and even change their names to Western ones. Often they were severed from their indigenous roots, culture, and community altogether. All things had become new, but people were rarely being taught to embody the way of Jesus through loving their enemies, caring for the Samaritan-like other, liberating the oppressed, and being peacemakers, all things Jesus actually taught. Indigenous Christians have often adopted these aspects of Jesus' ministry subversively and despite the emphasis of the Western missionary church.

This was all doable because Jesus himself had been converted into a Western European male. That's right: Jesus' image was forced to conform to our white supremacist arrangement. Especially prominent in America are the images of, and belief in, a white Jesus. European nations had reenvisioned Jesus through a Western and white prism rather than through Jesus' own Jewish body, culture, and background. Jesus only makes sense as a Messiah in Scripture through the story of Abraham, Moses, David, and the prophets. According to Jesus in Luke 24, the Hebrew Scriptures (particularly the Mosaic books and the Prophets) all concern him!

So why was Jesus, the poor Messiah from Galilee, transformed into a white man? Well, if Jesus is the revelation of God and the clearest picture of who God is, then his image has powerful significance. In transforming Jesus (both physically and culturally) into a white man, people of European descent gained a controlling interpretive grip not only on Jesus but also on the God revealed in Christ, and therefore on all the church.

---

8. Willie James Jennings, *The Christian Imagination: Theology and the Origins of Race* (New Haven, CT: Yale University Press, 2010), 286.

It is no wonder that European countries took up similar and troubling national ventures after the Protestant Reformation. England led the way in global conquest. Germany eventually synchronized Christianity with Germanic nationalism to the extent that the church easily fell susceptible to Nazism. America engaged in conquest and slavery, all because of the belief in its divinely manifested destiny. In each case, however, each modern Western nation began to identify its own national project as being divinely chosen to be the "New Israel." Everyone thought that they had claim on Jesus and God's will and were now the saviors to the world.

Combine that Western savior complex with a dominant cultural group with real power and you have a recipe for social disaster. Dominant groups anywhere in the world are prone to overriding the narratives of marginalized people with their own perspectives. A popular African proverb articulates it perfectly: "Until the story of the hunt is told by the lion, the tale of the hunt will always glorify the hunter." And with social power and position, a dominant group is uniquely able to marginalize other voices. They take for granted their own ideas and perspectives because they are backed by a majority. From there they lose sight of the fact that their particular view is just as socialized and contextualized as everyone else's. Not keeping sight of their own specific cultural influences leads to assuming that their views are "universal," "right," "neutral," and "objective." The development of whiteness grew out of a people who saw themselves as benevolent saviors to the world. Then, having consolidated enough national might to act on it, they went out and conquered other people. They did all this while continuing to see their own group as innocent in the midst of ongoing oppression and violence, and they believed they had a universal standpoint from which to objectively label the rest of the world.

These assumptions run directly against Christian practice and teaching, which affirm humanity's finiteness, limitedness, and the fact that we can now only see dimly. Dominant groups are always in danger of thinking that their perspective is synonymous with God's perspective. They frequently lack the humility to question their own ways and to be vulnerably open to the marginalized people in their society.

If dominant groups tend to universalize their norms, and if they sense that they are God's divinely elected nation, then you can expect overconfidence in interpreting social realities. I believe this overconfidence is one of the main reasons that white Christians were some of the loudest advocates for slavery and Jim Crow as they are today for black and brown incarceration, anti-immigration reform, and the labeling of most practicing Muslims as "terrorists." Often it has been the small, outsider white Christian traditions that have at least partly perceived some of these failures in white perception. This was true of the Mennonites and Quakers of Pennsylvania in 1688, who wrote the first petition against slavery.

We haven't yet realized how dangerous it is to conform our lives and our minds to the patterns of this world. And we don't yet know what it will require to have our lives transformed and our minds renewed. Until we do, many in the church will lead the way in "white is right" thinking.

## WHITE IDENTITY

Having significant conversations around white supremacy and racism with other Christian leaders who are deeply engaged in anti-racism work is valuable to me. During the writing of this book, I had one such opportunity. I was invited to gather with about three hundred Christian leaders engaged in a variety of faith-based justice work in the United States and around the world. Some were particularly invested in issues related to immigration, some committed their lives to issues of war and violence around the world, and others tackled sexual violence and patriarchy or fought for livable wages for people struggling to get by. It was great to be around all these folks who took up the call "to act justly and to love mercy" in all that they did (Micah 6:8 NIV). I was particularly glad that there was going to be an invitation-only lunch convening to discuss racism and racial justice work.

About fifty people gathered together in a room. I was grateful to be in the room to hear the wisdom from civil rights veterans like C. T. Vivian, and to rub shoulders with young activists from Ferguson and Baltimore who have been at the center of our current movement. I met folks who have been quietly working in their neighborhoods, as well as popular pastors who have inspired thousands of others. The conversation that we had was wide ranging. We had small table talk and shared stories. We let our elders pass on the wisdom that they had to those of us coming up. We also had a pretty lively discussion around the meaning of whiteness and its incompatibility with Christian orientations. It was great to be in the room, and to participate in a conversation where we were not trying to explain the basics of racism. Instead, we were having fairly advanced conversations around what it means to follow Jesus in our moment, considering white supremacy's present challenges and the obstacles before us.

When I left the conversation, I felt good. I had walked out of the room and into the hall when I was stopped by one of the attendees of our racial justice conversation. She was a middle-aged white woman, one of the few white people in the room. Most of the conversation partners were black, brown, Native American, and Asian. She asked me if I had a moment, and of course I said, "Sure." We sat down on a bench and she proceeded to ask me how I thought the conversation went. I might have hesitated with an answer, probably not sure how to respond to that vague question, but she immediately followed up with a more clarifying inquiry. She asked, "What did you think about how people were saying that white people couldn't be Christian?"

That isn't exactly what people were saying, but I knew what comments she was referring to.

Beginning with some basic concepts, I explained that whiteness is a social construction. If you go back to the fourteenth century, you can't find anyone identifying a people group as white. Whiteness, I explained, was created for the purpose of consolidating power and dominance over other people groups. Hence, as a social construction, whiteness is specifically about domination and violence.

As I was explaining these ideas, tears began rolling down her cheek. It became very clear to me at this point that she didn't belong in the advanced conversation on race that we were having. She was just a beginner, even though she had come thinking she was ready to participate and contribute. Her response revealed a common response that many white people express when confronted with racial realities: extreme fragility and sensitivity. Sometimes this fragility comes out in defensiveness, anger, and outright dismissal rather than crying. Either way, it reflects a deep discomfort with encountering even basic conversations on race. These conversations were far from her normal day-to-day life.

Rather than treat her like a child unable to deal with these important conversations, I decided to dig deeper. I explained that part of the reason that she was crying was because her identity was deeply but unknowingly intertwined with whiteness. If she didn't identify so deeply with whiteness, then my explanation of how and why whiteness was developed would not have been so troubling to her soul. Therefore, I followed up by explaining that she really didn't belong in the room with the others and that she had a lot of work to do to catch up to where she ought to be in conversations around race and racism. She nodded in agreement. She admitted that she wasn't as far along as she thought she was and that she needed to do a lot more self-study and self-reflection around white supremacy and her own identity.

Later in the day I found out from someone else that, indeed, she wasn't even invited to be part of the invitation-only conversation on race in the first place. I found the whole experience telling of how whiteness works in society. Not respecting the space for people of color and trusted allies to come together, encourage one another, and challenge one another is typical. Assuming that one's intrusion into an uninvited space is harmless and innocent is a common routine. Also, whiteness has people enter spaces presuming they know everything about a community even though they have never studied the people group and its concerns in depth. This often results in the feelings and experiences of the white person becoming the central focus, displacing the concerns of people of color who have been suffering under white supremacy for centuries.

This woman cared deeply about doing justice; otherwise she wouldn't have been there at all. She was open and teachable, so I pray that she continues to grow and learn. Like most white people, she needs to do the hard work of understanding race and racism's development in our country. Particularly, she needs to learn what it means for her to identify with whiteness and participate in white dominant society while claiming to follow Jesus. Performing and identifying with whiteness ends when we drop everything to be with our Christ.

## NAMING THE POWERS

In this chapter I have tried to do the simple, prophetic task of naming the powers at work in our world. Our society is structured in hierarchy in such a way that whiteness has mattered most. Though it is common for white people, especially white evangelicals, to talk about being colorblind, there is often no hesitation to speak about black problems. This turns our attention away from the social construction of whiteness. Racial terms are commonly used in white rhetoric. Race isn't actually avoided, but discussion about racism is. When race is talked about in white dominant culture, naming and discussing the life of people of color (and often their problems) is the extent of racial talk. There isn't much room for discussing whiteness, whether historically or in its present sociological form.

Jesus himself has been distorted and then employed to do work in oppressive systems. Of course, the true living and resurrected one is not the manipulated Jesus, who has endorsed violence and oppression for centuries. God, who is reconciling the world back to God's self, was revealed in a particular Form and in a particular Way. The Form and Way are that of Jesus of Nazareth, who invited people to repent from the old social order and to turn toward God's kingdom by following after him. Jesus emptied himself and took on human form.

And yet it was not a universal form, according to Paul; it was the embodiment of a slave. Jesus aligned himself with and called to himself a people among "the least of these." The "called-out ones" of Jesus (*ekklesia*) were gathered from the margins of society, from which a new community could be fashioned. Of course, Jesus invited the rich and the powerful to repent as well, and to join what God was doing, but for them this meant a radical reorientation of life. This new community would be distinct because, according to Jesus, it embodied a different kind of life from that of the Roman oppressors. The Romans "lord over" others, but "it must not be this way" for Jesus' followers (Matthew 20:25-26). To follow Jesus meant to renounce domination and alignment with the worldly powers. Instead, people who followed Jesus exemplified justice, mercy, and faithfulness in their lives, the weightier matters in the Scriptures that are often neglected (Matthew 23:23).

In America, whiteness matters, but not so among God's church, a distinct and alternative community. Following the crucified Christ radically aligns the church with those of low position in society (Romans 12:16). Following the crucified Christ isn't about ignoring the social meaning of crucifixion; rather, it recognizes that Jesus joined the thousands of Jews who were crucified by Roman powers during the first century.

In this, God has invited us all to come alongside the crucified of every time and place. From that vulnerable space, the Spirit renews our minds and transforms our lives to understand God's power and wisdom. This has nothing to do with the dominant way of seeing things, and everything to do with following Jesus. For the church, what matters most is not whiteness but the revelation of God found in Jesus' body, life, teaching, death, and resurrection as detailed in Scripture and encountered in Spirit. This means that white Christians must renounce the desire to control other people's lives and must reject the innocent savior complex, which sees everyone but oneself as in need of transformation. When deliverance and intervention is needed, the church looks to God.

# 6

# BLACK LIVES MATTER

Every day I live with the realities that come with being a young black male. I live with the irrational fear, the stereotypes, the clutched purses. I live with the perpetual threat of being suspected for a crime because I'm black at the wrong time or place, which is technically anytime that cops are looking for a black body to fit their description. In chapter 1, I told the story of the time that my brother was arrested because he "fit the description." That can happen to any young black man, anywhere, at almost any time.

Being black is draining. Blackness continues to be described pejoratively in America. Black skin in our world has been designated as a marker for all things bad. To be a black American is to have to constantly tell yourself that you are somebody, that you are made in the image of God, that you are creative and intelligent. Not doing so will result in drowning in the oceans of negative words about your existence and "your kind."

According to dominant culture, we are lazy, irresponsible, culturally depraved, lacking in morals, and our own worst enemies. Through white-controlled news media organizations like Fox News, CNN, and MSNBC, through most television and movies, and through everyday advertising campaigns and common cultural ideas, black people's humanity is constantly and unmercifully under assault. Assailing the character of black people through the use of these overarching blanket stereotypes is a common and accepted practice.

Static and overarching definitions of what it means to be black have justified the brutal controlling and killing of black life. It justified 246 years of dehumanizing and death-dealing legalized slavery. This was followed by a long season of new forms of white supremacist terrorism, including more than five thousand lynchings of black men, women, and children. This season also included the convict leasing system, which re-enslaved well over one hundred thousand black people until 1945 for "crimes" like vagrancy, not getting a white person's permission to change employment, or talking to or having sex with a white woman.[1] That is just the tip of the iceberg of our twentieth-century white supremacist past.

But our present situation has also created violent forms of white control and execution of black bodies. This occurs through antiblack sentiments that are consumed uncritically. Transnational media corporations and popular political and government leaders push black stereotypes through white power structures, creating the foundation for our current wars against poor, black inner-city neighborhoods. For example, Philadelphia, my city, has allowed for the massive defunding of public education in poor black and brown communities. This has resulted in the shutting down of public schools all over the city—at the very same time that state funding is directed toward the privatized and lucrative prison-industrial complex. This is what many in my community more simply label "the school-to-prison pipeline."

Michelle Alexander has done helpful work in getting the message of such dire realities out to broader society, and she has directly engaged Christian communities and organizations willing to listen. In her book, *The New Jim Crow*, she couples her legal expertise with deep research and narrates the problem of mass incarceration in our society. She explains that in just the few decades after the civil rights movement, America's prison population exploded from about three hundred thousand to more than

1. Douglas A. Blackmon, *Slavery by Another Name: The Re-Enslavement of Black Americans from the Civil War to World War II* (New York: Doubleday, 2008), 53–54.

two million inmates.[2] These numbers make incarceration practices in countries like China and Russia, which Americans often see as restrictive, to be much less overbearing than the United States. More problematic is that this explosion has grown disproportionately at the expense of black and brown communities, which have been targeted through official policies. It is racial minorities who are most stigmatized and most targeted. Through the "war on drugs" campaign, which has used colorblind rhetoric to cover its trail, black men (and increasingly black women) have been racially profiled, arrested, and locked in cages. Few seem to recognize that there is an ongoing racial terrorism that continues to unfold in and against black communities in the twenty-first century, resulting in one out of every three black young men going through the judicial system at some point in his life because of nonviolent drug charges. As Alexander and many other researchers have revealed, black youth and white youth are using drugs at comparable rates, with white youth actually having a slightly higher level of use.

In these and countless other ways, the black psyche has been routinely attacked and crushed in our society. This subject rarely gets talked about. We have not fully taken account of the manner in which four hundred years of constant, persistent, and devastating antiblack ideology has crippled our ability to even understand the depth of what has happened in this land. Some black people may say otherwise, but if you watch common interactions, you will see the internalizing of these racial ideologies in subtle expressions of white trust and simultaneous antiblack prejudice. Our intuitive responses, in our everyday interactions, expose the power of these hegemonic ideas, which certainly have mutated but still have not quit their assault on black humanity.

Racist ideology doesn't just result in black people not loving other black people; it also attacks one's own self-perception. Inside my own ears are the soft whispers saying that I am not good enough, that I am not beautiful, that I do not deserve to be loved, that my culture is backward, and that I do not belong in certain spaces. To be black in America is to embody flesh that has

2. Michelle Alexander, *The New Jim Crow: Mass Incarceration in the Age of Color-blindness* (New York: The New Press, 2012), 6.

been marked by white people for four hundred years as despised, immoral, improper, threatening, and in need of white supervision. Too often in the black community either we accept the antiblack sentiments as definitive statements of our essence or, as we will explore more in chapter 7, we respond just as negatively by seeking to become everything "good" according to the standard of white features, values, and culture.

Part of the creative black struggle to live into who God created us to be has always meant fighting the overbearing message that we are not a people worthy of love. The black church has been an important space in which battles with these evil forces and ideologies have been engaged. However, the black church has struggled through this, not always having the courage to dissent from mainstream voices with enough clarity, strength, and wisdom. The black church has work to do.

That I must also name and discuss the white church and its monumental failure in this area is one of the great tragedies of American Christian history. The white church—and there certainly is such a thing—has often been silent in response to the four hundred years of assault on black humanity. At times it has outright taken the lead in antiblack racism. The white church has too often failed to see each and every black life as beloved by God, not reducible to static stereotypes like "thug" or "welfare queen." That the white Christian community has allowed these powerful myths to crush the most vulnerable among us calls into question the degree to which the crucified one has been at the center of the church.

In the church, everyone from every background must recognize that black people ought to be loved and valued, because we too are made in the image of God. The church must stand up and affirm that black people matter. Unfortunately, while all lives should matter, black life has not mattered much in America. In this chapter we will remember precisely how black people have not mattered in everyday life. This is a call for the church to take seriously the antiblack ideology and sentiments that are so pervasive in our country. Loving others we have been socialized to devalue should be a familiar practice for the church. We ought to be a community discipled into loving socially rejected people as our heavenly Father does.

## HISTORICAL ASSAULTS ON BLACK IDENTITY

During slavery, African American humanity was assaulted with precision. Moderate estimates place the number at about 12.5 million Africans who were captured and brought to the New World. Enslaved Africans were not only told that they were inferior and divinely appointed to work for white masters, but were also accused of being lazy. That's right: white people who had stolen labor from millions of Africans through racialized violence had the audacity to call my ancestors lazy. When white masters tortured and raped black women, they claimed that it was black women who were the pathologically hypersexual beings. From the beginning, popular antiblack sentiment was used to veil racial violence and justify practices and policies that allowed white people to treat Africans terribly while not disrupting the white sense of innocence.

Assaulting black people's humanity did two things. First, it attempted to make black people accept their lot in life. They had been told who they are, and through constant psychological bombardment, they slowly began to partially accept these definitions. Antiblackness terrorized black psyches and self-esteems and bolstered confidence in the dominant group, social systems, and structures of society. This worked at times. But just as importantly, most slaves resisted these totalizing claims of who they were.

Second, as stated earlier, antiblack sentiment had an important role in white dominant culture too. With these stereotypes activated, whites were able to justify their actions based on their concocted ideas of black humanity. Antiblack ideology was the engine that allowed white supremacy to continue without white people in each new generation perceiving their own actions as inhumane and heinous. As long as black people were themselves the problem—a problem that needed to be controlled by white society—then the white dominant group could continue claiming innocence for the social realities that existed. No guilt, lament, or repentance is necessary when you tell yourself that people are simply getting what they deserve.

Black people have been property and sexual objects controlled and dominated by the white majority's whims throughout our history. In earlier times we were nothing but "niggers" or "jezebels." Today racism is often much more coded and disguised. Instead of using actual racial language that is explicitly and overtly anti-black, American rhetoric has become more sophisticated. Now categories like "thug" and "welfare queen" are thrown around to question the humanity, worth, and life of black people. At first you might not think of these terms as racial terms, but just watching the popular usage of these terms unveils their racist underbelly. These terms have been deployed consistently and with precision to create new stereotypes while avoiding all charges of racism. Race doesn't have to be explicitly mentioned at any point. This is why anytime there is a black victim, the media immediately begins a witch hunt for some moral failure, mistake, or misdemeanor. In that way, the media can appropriate a coded term reserved mostly for black life.

With the killing of Trayvon Martin, for example, much white energy was spent trying to criminalize this child, digging into his background in the hopes of finding skeletons in his closet. Instead of giving attention to the racial profiling that set that moment off, and the grown man with a long string of violent assaults before and after that terrible night, observers constantly called Martin a "thug." This is no different than what we have seen more recently with Michael Brown, Eric Garner, and others. Blackness is always assumed to be the problem. White American news reporters have a maddening and unexplainable desire to qualify a black person's humanity. We all have failures because we are all human and all have fallen short of the *imago Dei* found in Jesus Christ. This understanding of human nature seems to be absent from these reports, which solely want to criminalize blackness and defend the image of whiteness whenever possible.

## DOLL EXPERIMENTS

After graduating from college, I began to immediately supplement my education. The problem wasn't with what I was taught but with what I was *not* taught. Given that I only had marginal engagement with African American scholars and thinkers in my undergraduate program, I dived into the well of African American literature. I read black theologians, critical race thinkers, sociologists, and philosophers, as well as Christians of all races who were writing on racial reconciliation. During that time I also found myself wanting to get a better hold on African American history, especially the civil rights movement. I attended a nine-day civil rights bus tour that traveled from Pennsylvania, down through the South, and back. During that time we visited key sites and met with and listened to many people who had participated in the southern freedom movement, several of whom knew Martin Luther King Jr. personally. This was a life-giving moment that opened my eyes to how the 1950s and 1960s protests fit into the larger struggle and resistance of African Americans since the seventeenth century.

During my self-study and reeducation, I came across the now famous mid-twentieth-century Clark doll experiments.[3] For those not familiar with this research, I'll give a brief synopsis. In these tests, young black and white children, one at a time, answered a series of questions. A white doll and a black doll sat in front of the child during the whole exercise. An interviewer would ask the child things like "Which doll is the good doll?" and "Which doll is the bad doll?" Other questions included "Which doll is the pretty doll?" and "Which doll is the ugly one?"

Given that this study was first conducted in the 1940s, we may not be completely surprised by the white children's answers. Overwhelmingly, the white children attributed all the positive attributes to the white doll and all the negative attributes to the black doll. Clearly, they had been deeply influenced by antiblack sentiments even at a very young age.

What some people might find surprising are the responses from the black children. The black children demonstrated high levels of prejudice as well. But unlike the popular idea of "reverse racism," which might have predicted that the black children would rate the white dolls more negatively than the black, the research

---

3. Kenneth B. Clark and Mamie P. Clark, "Emotional Factors in Racial Identification and Preference in Negro Children," *The Journal of Negro Education* 19, no. 3 (July 1, 1950): 341–50, doi:10.2307/2966491.

revealed something much more insidious. The racial prejudice of the young black children also revealed antiblack sentiments. The black kids were also inclined to attribute goodness and beauty to the white dolls and to think that the black dolls were bad and ugly. Antiblack sentiment was so powerful in American society that young black and white children had already internalized these cultural messages.

Even sadder than these old findings is the fact that this experiment has been repeated frequently since the turn of the twenty-first century and the findings are still the same: both white and black children are still predisposed to dislike blackness. Search online for "doll experiment race" to get a sample of the many experiments that have been done recently. The results of these studies should haunt our consciences and force us to evaluate how this can still be the case.

It was painful for me to watch the video of one of these experiments, in which young black children assign negative attributes to the black doll and then point to the same doll when asked, "Which doll looks most like you?" But I refuse to turn away from the problem at hand. The lack of honest engagement around how antiblack racism continues in our churches and the larger society will result in us having the same problems again and again going forward. The temptation to think that ignoring race (which is the historical approach of white dominant culture) will solve these problems leads only to the continuation of the vicious cycle. The urge to highlight reverse prejudice as the primary racial problem of our time misrepresents what is actually emblematic of the crisis in our society: black people and black life are not valued.

Going back to the founding of our country, blackness was deeply grounded with a theological sense of depravity. Joe Feagin explains it this way: "In Old English, the word 'black' meant sooted, while the word 'white' meant to gleam brightly, as for a candle. In line with earlier Christian usage, the word 'black' was used by the English colonists to describe sin and the devil."[4] Western societies' concepts around sin and heathenism were all trans-

---

4. Joe R. Feagin, *Racist America: Roots, Current Realities, and Future Reparations*, 3rd ed. (New York: Routledge, 2014), 68.

ferred onto dark-skinned African bodies. Blackness and whiteness, as they were constructed by Anglo-Saxon Protestants, became complete polar opposites. For whiteness to be supreme at the top of the racial hierarchy, blackness needed to be inferior and loathed at the bottom of the human ladder. Once again, Feagin explains this mind-set:

> This racial framing increasingly focused not only on the negative blackness of the others but also on the virtuous whiteness of Europeans. Africans and African Americans were viewed as physically, aesthetically, morally, and mentally inferior to whites—differences regarded as more or less permanent. "Whiteness" was created by self-named whites in opposition to "blackness," in comparison to which whiteness was not only different but quite superior. Significantly, the antiblack framing was not "out there," but rather in the white mind (brain) and riddled with racialized emotions.[5]

The truth to which we must open our eyes is that it's hard for all of us in the United States to truly love black people as fully created after the image of God. Antiblack racism has affected every community and people group around the globe. It has been passed through European colonialism and is still being pushed, though in updated forms, through antiblack stereotypes that pervade American media, which is exported and consumed all over the world. Antiblackness is everyone's problem. It influences people around the world to see dark skin as ugly, even among their own ethnic and racial groups. Whether we are talking about Africa, Asia, South America, or Europe, it is clear that antiblackness has infected people's perceptions of one another.

Dismantling the unconscious antiblack sentiment residing in us and our communities will require intentional commitment to love and stand with vulnerable black people. Affirming "Black Lives Matter" must always include all black lives. There is no doubt that black men, like me, are targeted and attacked just for being us. This must be addressed. Unfortunately, dealing with issues of racism often stops there. To say that black lives matter must include

---

5. Ibid., 68–69.

black women's lives too. They are also navigating our racialized society. I'll touch on this more in a later chapter, but for now let me just say that we must affirm the lives of everyone in the black community. Not just men, or those who dress well, or those who are highly educated or middle class.

We must also stand up for black LGBTQ people being bullied or marginalized in our neighborhoods. Too often I have heard Christians insist that in the church we are not homophobic, which is sometimes true but not always so. The black church is often portrayed as "backward" by white progressives and liberals. Yet it should be noted that it is the white Christian community that frequently produces groups like the vitriolic Westboro Baptist Church. White lenses are not necessarily helpful assessments, especially when considering that oppressed communities cannot simply trust the ethics of white liberals and progressives but instead must always work out their own ethics while following Jesus and dialoguing with other oppressed people groups. It seems like the true test of whether we are homophobic will be revealed in our ability to love our black LGBTQ neighbors, embodying mercy and justice when they are wronged, and standing in solidarity with them when they are mistreated. This is our Christian task and calling, whether or not your community differs or aligns with LGBTQ sexual ethics. Loving our neighbor, welcoming the excluded, and seeking first to listen and understand before speaking are basic Christian tenets that have often been ignored. Every black life must matter, from newborn baby to the elderly. Antiracism work must be done to affirm the value of everyone stigmatized by racial categories.

It is hard for all of us to affirm that each particular black life matters and has value before God. That's right. It is not just difficult for white people, but it is hard *even for black people* to see and love other black people the way God does.

## POOR BLACKS AS LIGHTNING RODS FOR ANTIBLACK ASSAULTS

It pains me when I hear people take cheap shots at poor black people. As I was writing this book, I had a conversation with someone who did just that. Nine times out ten when I have such encounters, the person offering the diatribe is a white, middle-class person who lives, moves, and breathes purely in white dominant culture. They have never lived in poor black neighborhoods, and they certainly do not have significant relationships with poor black people. Yet somehow their segregated life experience doesn't appear to be the slightest barrier to verbally abusing the most vulnerable citizens of this land. Apparently, actual firsthand experience or intimate relationship isn't a prerequisite for being an expert on black people's problems. Stereotypes from the media seem to be sufficient. Besides, poor black people are easy targets. People can say what they want, often have a laugh at their expense, and there will be no social consequences for such action. Poor black people have no champion to defend them socially or politically in the public square.

In high school, my family had fully crossed over into the black middle class. We moved to the 'burbs, and as I wrote about in chapter 2, I attended a middle-class suburban high school from grades ten through twelve. Since graduating college I have lived in black neighborhoods—first in Harrisburg, Pennsylvania, and then in Philadelphia—comprising mostly black poor and working-class families. However, my own household is most certainly middle class. I don't have to deal with the stress of wondering where my next meal is coming from or the stigma of not having a college degree while searching for a job. I have healthcare, food, housing, transportation, and a reliable and livable income. And soon, Lord willing, I will attain a PhD, which will give me serious advantages compared to most people within the black community. The life I live as a black male is navigated through a black middle-class experience.

Blackness by itself is tiring enough, but to be poor and black is a burden that I honestly can only sympathize with now. I've frequently had neighbors share with me their struggles to find work and provide for their families. Tirelessly they look for better opportunities to provide livable wages for themselves and their families, and often they are unable to. Yet it is precisely poor black families who are often the most popular targets of the media and the middle class. Through vitriol and stereotype, poor black families get blasted 24/7 for every aspect of their lives. Many middle-class

Americans want to micromanage these families' lives to the point
that some are concerned with whether poor people can buy sea-
food with their government assistance. (We wouldn't want poor
people to periodically enjoy and celebrate life!) Because blackness
and welfare have been merged together in many American's minds,
government assistance has been a ridiculous preoccupation in the
minds of dominant culture. Poor black people, it seems, are nothing but leeches who don't deserve a dime from anyone. Rather
than look at how our economy deeply and unjustly distributes
resources, people often describe poor black people as the source of
American economic issues. Poor black people are the scapegoats
of America. Who will champion them?

Yet what is amazing, and surely a sign that there is a God in the
world, is that many black folk courageously get up each morning
with a renewed determination to keep going. Through four hundred years of oppression, black people have defiantly lifted their
heads, put one foot in front of the other, and creatively struggled
to hold onto a deep hope for a better future. Black people continue
to create something out of nothing, stretch little into much, hustle,
grind, and make do with scraps. Can some families do better in
this area or that? Absolutely. I am a firm believer in calling for personal accountability and transformation. But what family couldn't
do better? Most folks who are so quick to blast poor black people
need to look in the mirror at the log in their eye rather than worry-
ing about the speck in someone else's. Some people's dysfunctions
are just hidden behind middle-class walls and are not the topic
of American evening news. I've seen white suburban families full
of all sorts of dysfunction and drama as well. So maybe it's time
to stop scapegoating the most vulnerable among us. There is one
person who is a champion for the poor and oppressed, and his
name is Jesus. He doesn't take kindly to those who trample over
the vulnerable.

## THE LENS OF THE CRUCIFIED CHRIST

Despite four hundred years of assault, black faith and resistance
has resulted in creative affirmations for our humanity, culture,
and creativity. We have dared to love one another and to reject

the dominant myths in our country. For centuries we have risked loving one another through mutual social and economic support. What is most amazing about our history is that, over and over again, black people have frequently not turned toward violent revolt. Such actions would seem to be reasonable responses to four hundred years of oppression. Instead, black people have primarily chosen to pursue love, justice, restoration, and healing. Most white people need to get past their faulty and insufficient understanding of black history and grasp even a fraction of the nonstop assault on black humanity that persists even to this day. If that happened, they would join the movement of God unfolding in history among the despised. Recognizing the strength, struggle, and courage of black people, despite unbending antiblack oppression, should lead white Christians into the posture of students to this Jesus-shaped tradition. That should be followed by thanks and gratitude for black people's transformative love, deep courage, and choice for restorative justice instead of retribution and revenge. Given American celebration of revolutionary wars, black people would have legitimate reason to take up arms. But black people have rarely chosen the American way. Instead, they have often demonstrated resilience in truth and grace toward the white dominant group—a way of life that looks more like the way of Jesus than anything else.

Black life as despised humanity runs parallel to the life of Christ, who entered into socially rejected and scandalized life. The question about this poor Jew from Nazareth living under Roman oppression—"Can anything good come out of Nazareth?" (John 1:46)—demonstrates the extent to which Jesus was seen as an insignificant and punishable body. His body was one that could be grabbed at night without recourse and then run through an unjust judicial process. Like the thousands of black bodies that hung from trees, having been executed by the hands of white mobs, Jesus' body was hung on that old rugged tree as a public spectacle of Rome. It was a death reserved for bandits and revolutionaries. That Jesus identified so intimately with "the wretched of the earth," even to the point of death, should result in God's church daring to see humanity from the perspective of God. To follow

Jesus every day demands that we also must dare to interpret vulnerable and outcast bodies through the lens of the crucified Christ, through whom God's wisdom and power is revealed.

The task for us as a church is to allow the resurrected Jesus to be present with us, inspiring us toward risky and controversial love, even when society tells us that the recipients of our love are not worthy. Just as Jesus affirmed the life of the outcast Samaritans of his day, so too must we risk concrete love through action that affirms black life and cares about how all black bodies are treated.

Following Jesus means never accepting and conforming to the sentiments and patterns of this world. It means being transformed after the image of the Son, taking on a renewed mind that is no longer socialized by and indistinguishable from dominant society. Despite popular rhetoric around reverse racism in race relations between black and white people, the issue has never been whether most black people are capable of seeing white people as truly human and worthy of love. We willfully ignore the reality of internalized antiblack ideology and racial hierarchy when we make that the issue. *The real challenge in America is whether both white and black people are willing to subversively risk loving black people as though each life were created by God.* The church, to whom God is revealed through the crucified Christ, has the key that unlocks the answers to our problems and the type of concrete, loving action and speech that is needed. The church in particular needs to be an alternative community that demonstrates to the world that truly loving all God's people—especially those we are socialized to believe don't matter—is possible.

# 7

# THE LURE OF STATUS AND RESPECT

I've always been proud to have been raised during the second generation of hip-hop. My formative growing-up years were the 1990s, and I naturally think we were the greatest generation. That is an unbiased and objective assessment, of course. And while I have a lot of respect for the earliest pioneers of 1970s and '80s hip-hop, I find my generation's music to be of a superior quality. We didn't create hip-hop, but we took it to another level. The lyricism of the '90s puts the pop rap hits of today to shame. I know; I'm showing my age!

Some of my favorite artists growing up included Nas, Biggie, Heavy D, DMX, The LOX, Tupac, the Fugees, and yes, even some Mase (I know I just lost some credibility). I certainly preferred an East Coast hip-hop flavor, which mattered back then, though I did own a tape of Warren G (he was from the East Coast but had a distinctly West Coast sound). My older brother, for whatever reason, listened to a lot of West Coast hip-hop. We actually only owned a few tapes back then, purchased without the knowledge of my parents. (Sorry, Mom and Dad. Love ya!) So we used to get cassettes of music we didn't like and put tape over the holes so that we could record over them.

In Philly, one of the longest running hip-hop stations was and still is Power 99. On weekdays in the evening, Power 99 would have the "9 at 9." These were the most popular songs of the day played in order, from least to most popular, beginning right at 9:00 p.m. This was a prime time for my creative genius to get select songs off the radio to create a mixtape. This was standard hip-hop procedure. And after you filled up your tape, it was your duty to brag about how hot your mixtape was!

In the late '90s, one popular song that got a lot of play was "Money, Power & Respect" by The LOX. The song was not necessarily the most lyrically creative, nor did it have the most depth of insight, but it did tap into a common desire. There were no unexpected twists with this one. Put simply, the song was about getting money, power, and respect. According to the song, first you get the money, then you get the power, and then finally you have respect. These things are, according to The LOX, "the key to life." I still remember how many adults were quick to criticize the song for being superficial and shallow. Looking back, I wonder if that critique was premature.

I am not suggesting that the adults who were critical of this song were wrong about a shallow message. Of course money, power, and respect are not the keys to life! However, I wonder if some of the adults in the black community, as well as the broader American society, were being as honest and transparent about their own desires and pursuits as The LOX were, given the actual choices many people make. The American way is, at root, about the pursuit of happiness by chasing after money, power, and respect. The LOX were not introducing new concepts to American culture; they were merely adopting the philosophy that had permeated our society for centuries. "Money, power, respect" is a fundamentally American doctrine. The LOX, in this song, merely put a black aspirational twist on an old and familiar tune. The song holds a mirror to dominant society's internal motivations and exposes the real lure these dominant cultural values have on those within subcultures of American life. All of American society is enticed by the American trinity of money, power, and respect.

The forces at work in our culture that define the good life in America are hidden from the awareness of most Americans. Christians are not an exception. Our inability to discern the mold that our lives are unconsciously being formed into, or judged against, doesn't make that mold any less a reality. Social hierarchy enables a people group to make their values and norms dominant. Whether consciously or unconsciously, we are all being pulled by the magnetism of dominant cultural norms around what a respectable life looks like.

People of color living as minorities in the United States are not above the powerful images of what is "respectable." In fact, it is precisely those who have been left out, denied full participation in society, and excluded from authentic power sharing and decision making who deeply yearn for acceptance. The lack of societal affirmation can create unhealthy attempts to pursue standing in society. Then, before we know it, we are unconsciously reaffirming the very standards that crushed our ancestors. Rather than renouncing the way society marginalizes people, racial minorities can uncritically adopt the very ideological perspectives created by dominant culture. These perspectives indirectly perpetuate injustice in our country and around the world.

In this chapter we'll consider the ways that the doctrine of respectability plays itself out in communities that have lived under a dominating power. Then we'll look at the ways that Christ's life and Paul's words, both in the context of life under an oppressors' rule, challenge all of us to stop conforming to the patterns of this world.

## THE RESIDUE OF IMPERIALISM

In the summer of 2011, I had the opportunity to spend some time in Kenya. That trip has left lasting imprints on my mind, impressions that offer perspective in my current thinking. I still remember my group's thirteen-hour layover in London on our way to Kenya. This was my first (and still only) time in Europe. Our layover was long enough that we were able to leave the airport and tour the city for half the day.

Our group enjoyed being taken around this world-famous city and exploring sights you would expect to visit in such a tour. (Sadly, I found out that the London Bridge is *not* falling down, contrary to what I had been taught by nursery rhymes.) Fighting off some serious jet lag and lack of sleep from our flight, we ventured out to historic palaces, churches, bridges, and so forth. Practically all the architectural monuments we visited had significant history for England's imperial legacy. While touring, we tried to blend in—as much as a large group of black Americans can in London.

Eventually it was time to go, so we headed back to the airport. I don't remember too much about the remaining flights. Our final destination was the airport in Mombasa, Kenya, and I still vividly remember leaving the airport grounds. Almost immediately after getting off the airport property, our view was of countless shacks across the countryside. During our hour-long drive to our temporary residence, we saw what seemed like never-ending poverty. I have encountered people living in tough conditions before, but not the same quantity of people over miles and miles of land. In the West Indies, for example, I had seen shantytowns, but there one would also periodically pass through middle-class areas. As we drove out through Mombasa, for a while it seemed as if there were no middle class at all. It was more than halfway through the week until we saw an upper-class neighborhood. The ratio of poverty to wealth was beyond what I had ever been exposed to before.

As I looked out the van window at the unending conditions that masses of black people live in, I kept going back to London, where we just had been tourists. In London we saw palaces, grandiose churches, and the residue of a generational legacy of imperial wealth. Kenya had been a British colony up until the 1960s, my new Kenyan friend John reminded me. It became very clear how direct a connection there was between the wealth and infrastructure in London and the poverty endured by many of the Kenyan people.

Though I had expected just another tourist experience in London, the layover, in fact, became my teacher. My short stay there offered a historical reminder for me of the connection between power and poverty, wealth and suffering. Rarely do we think of wealth in such ways, especially in America. This is odd, because in America, power, land, and wealth were gained directly by stealing the land of the indigenous people and stealing the bodies and labor of Africans for several centuries. American wealth, power, and respect were built through domination and violence, realities that many conveniently forget or avoid considering.

This issue kept coming back to me while in Kenya. We were in Kenya for Madaraka Day, the celebration of independence from the British. It was easier to be drawn in by the lure of London when considering it outside of its historical context. Once you remember that its pretty, shiny buildings were gained through Britain's imperial conquest all around the globe, its seduction diminishes quickly.

Of course, as an outsider I could see some things about the lure of power and dominance that some of my new Kenyan friends were not as quick to see. On one day, I had the pleasure of speaking at a gathering of Christian young adults in the city of Mombasa. After the meeting, as we did after every event (no matter if it was burning hot in the midday or cooling off in the evening), we drank hot tea. I found it to be a small but noticeable British imprint on Kenyan culture.

That same evening, a few of us were in a circle talking about cultural differences and quirks, as well as global politics. While I was impressed by my new Kenyan friends' insight into global politics, I found myself differing on one specific cultural observation of American life. Particularly, one of the young women noted that they as Kenyans spoke "proper" English and that they did so much better than Americans. This is a popular point, one I had heard before ever going to Kenya. In a similar fashion, I have heard both white and black Americans critique poor, black, urban or rural Americans for not speaking "properly." So there, with my Kenyan friends, I questioned the logic of what made some language proper and some language illegitimate. My point—which I have also made during discussions of black vernacular in America—is that those who violently colonized you ought not set the standard of what is proper and respectable.

In the case of my Kenyan friends, I think they shouldn't judge themselves as right or wrong based on the standard of the British system still hanging over them. They must be free to make the language their own. Of course, I am not suggesting that they shouldn't learn any dominant cultural languages, because life survival doesn't make that a helpful option. Yet to name a particular type of speech "proper" or "right" is to maintain an arbitrary standard set by those who formerly dominated their people. The British way ought not to be the pattern to which they should forever seek to conform. Those with power should not make linguistic and cultural differences into moral judgments, diminishing the creativity of people who have survived their oppression. Saying "ain't" instead of "is not," for example, has nothing to do with morality and ethics; supposedly "proper" speech is simply a manifestation of the power of the dominant group that universalizes its norms. Those living on the margins must be critical of the definitions of right and wrong by those who have influence over society to make their own logic seem inherently right and good.

The residue of British colonization remains in Kenyan culture. It is impossible for any people who have been colonized or oppressed to not feel the lure of those in power. While it was easier for me as an outsider to see what was at stake in Kenya, I also know that America has socialized me as well, in ways that I am oblivious to. Furthermore, dominant culture often conforms us toward an image of American respect and status that deeply contradicts Jesus' image. And yet Jesus promises an alternative to the imperial imprint that tries to determine our values and practices; that alternative is the kingdom of God.

## THE DOCTRINE OF RESPECTABILITY

Black people in America have a long history of trying to find acceptance by conforming to the norms of the oppressive and dominant group. For the black community of the past, the doctrine of respectability was a complex mixture of practical self-determination, commitment to the "uplift of the race," and the hope that playing by the rules might prove to whites how civilized they were so that they would stop oppressing them, lynching them, segregating them, and denying their humanity.

Those who held to the doctrine of respectability hoped that the trajectory of white supremacy would shift if black behavior changed. This framework looked at everything from the perspective of "the negro problem." Black behavior was the critical element to keep track of and improve. During slavery, slave owners insisted that slaves were "lazy" and needed harsh correction and oversight. The problem was thought to be black behavior, not the oppressive and violent form of slavery that white people practiced.

This concern about black behavior characterized the mid-twentieth century as well. The focus was not on white domination, the Ku Klux Klan, and White Citizens' Council terrorism, or on the unequal Jim Crow society that kept black people under racial domination. Rather, attention was on whether black people were becoming "civilized" and "respectable" enough.

Portions of the African American community, like most ethnic minority groups in America, still espouse a doctrine of respectability. Today, when we discuss issues around mass incarceration and police brutality, too often the conversation turns toward how black people should act: pulling up pants, taking out earrings, and speaking "properly," as if such behavior merits being treated as less than human. In the early twenty-first century, Bill Cosby went on tour to critique black people for not living up to the standards of white dominant culture. While some of his points were about personal responsibility, much of it was about dominant cultural respectability. He even at times made fun of African Americans' names. As we've seen, this mind-set, as deeply colonized as it was, has a long history.

Similarly, some black leaders denigrate hip-hop music and tattoos as if they were the primary issues related to the black community's well-being. They seem to think that if we could just fit in with dominant society more, the four hundred years of white oppression against us would suddenly erode. Certainly the testimonies of many black middle-class women and men—about hitting glass ceilings, driving while black, or being followed in gated communities—offer just a few examples that the solution is not a doctrine of respectability.

Kanye West touched on this issue of oppressed peoples accepting dominant culture in one of his early albums. In a song called "All Falls Down," West transparently discusses his struggles as an African American with adopting all societal messages. He suggests that black people, like whites, sometimes buy things not because they need them but to cover up internal longings. He goes as far as saying that "they made us hate ourself and love they wealth."[1]

What is brilliant about these particular lines is that they unveil the internalized antiblack racism and materialism that are so common, and how deeply intertwined these are with black pursuits for justice and freedom. Unless the church can match and exceed this level of transparency, while turning toward gospel transformation through a renewing of our minds, we are doomed to be puppets of hidden and powerful forces.

## DO NOT BE CONFORMED

People generally either affirm or subvert the standards of dominant society. Realistically speaking, many of us engage in a mixture of the two. Few churches discuss the ways that Christian communities also participate in these acts of affirmation or resistance. People of color, despite popular opinion, are not absolved from this reality. As people of color, we can be deeply seduced by the dominant culture, and we frequently conform to its patterns much more than we have acknowledged to ourselves and to one another.

Romans 12:1-2 is, somewhat strangely, one of the most memorized and quoted passages in Western Christianity. But I am not sure if the American church has considered the radical implications of this Pauline teaching. Paul knew what it was to live under imperial rule. The Roman way of life was a dominant force that could not be ignored. Rome's occupational presence was so great that it can only be talked about as one of the largest empires in history. Its political power and cultural influence were so vast that its values and standards could easily be taken for granted as the only right way. In that world, it appeared as though Caesar was

---

1. Kanye West, "All Falls Down," *The College Dropout* (New York: Roc-A-Fella Records/Hip Hop: Manufactured and marketed by The Island Def Jam Music Group; distributed by Universal Music & Video Distribution Corp., 2004).

lord. Each territory that was violently claimed through military conquest was intentionally set up to imitate Rome. The governmental powers extended all the way to local presence and privileges in each region. Those whose necks were under the foot of Rome probably often felt they had very few options but to play by Roman rules.

What do you do when another people group with proven military strength dominates you? What do you do when its cultural hegemony erodes one's own culture and values? What do you do when you are being drawn into the very systems and societal patterns that are also taxing, exploiting, humiliating, and executing you on a regular basis? The uncritical or despair-filled stance is to adopt an "if you can't beat them, join them" mentality.

Paul, however, takes a more subversive posture: "I exhort you, brothers and sisters, by the mercies of God, to present your bodies as a sacrifice—alive, holy, and pleasing to God—which is your reasonable service. Do not be conformed to this present world, but be transformed by the renewing of your mind, so that you may test and approve what is the will of God—what is good and well-pleasing and perfect" (Romans 12:1-2).

These two verses challenge us with an embodied, decolonizing way of life that refuses to join the oppressive systems that manage and puppet most people's lives. First, we are told that we must put our very bodies, through action, on the line. Our bodies must become living sacrifices. Our bodies, and what we do with them, actually matter. We are not disembodied souls, and God cares about more than our spiritual lives. God says, Put your body on the line! What kind of bodily life will you engage in? Will your body be aligned with the rituals of American civil religion? Or will you vulnerably place your body in confrontation with the establishment, as Jesus did with his own body when he flipped tables in judgment of the injustice and idolatry in the temple? Apparently such bodily involvement is our reasonable service to God.

Paul, however, isn't just talking about embodiment in general. He is writing specifically about his readers' desire to respond to the dominant patterns of Roman society. Again, at that time people would have taken for granted the idea that Roman standards *nedanastive sbcvcr*

were right. The Roman Empire was so powerful that it got to write the story of itself, from a position of dominance, and actually have that perspective stick. Much like claims about American exceptionalism or the American dream, Roman way of life under the reign of Caesar was propagated as salvific. Different people groups and regions just needed to align with the ever-expanding kingdom. They needed to get with the program.

Paul's message, however, is *not* to go with the flow. His challenge for the church is to *not* conform to the patterns of society. Do not just go along with what seems right to the reasoning of those in power, Paul suggests—those who disseminate their views through all the "proper" and "official" channels. Their governing role does not translate into the ethical way of life of God's kingdom centered in Jesus' ongoing presence and shaped after the form of his life, teachings, death, and resurrection. The revelation of Jesus, and his significance for the church, clashes with the reasoning of dominant society. Nonconformity is the message: nonconformity in our bodies, nonconformity in our minds, and nonconformity in our ways of being in the world.

Very rarely do we take time in the church to consider how our minds have been colonized by the current social order. Minorities are not absolved of this challenge. On one hand, oppressed communities do often perceive and work at things in creative and subversive ways—ways that open them up to see with greater clarity the patterns that shape everyday life. On the other hand, a sense of societal neglect and a desire for dominant cultural participation can lead the same people to become uncritical students of status quo mind-sets.

It is true that Christian disciples ought to be culturally intelligent and able to engage various types of people. The danger is when we adopt the worldview and framework of the dominant society wholesale. Instead, Christians must engage in the harder work of deciphering how and what to use from this bank of knowledge. Knowledge is never neutral, and how we use it is also a moral and ethical issue. Knowledge that is wielded to align with oppressive power is intellectually unethical in its usage.

We must wrestle with making our every thought align with the truth of Jesus—the executed, resurrected Christ who sustains all life and who reconciles all things. This demands, as Paul explains, a renewing of our minds. The church is being transformed from dominant, conformed, and colonized perspectives so that the members of the body can see what God is doing in the world. What we will find, as Paul did, is that what God is up to looks nothing like what the Roman Empire or America is up to. Empires are not saviors of the world. They are the old patterns that are temporal and that will eventually pass away.

Nonconformist ways of exploring the world mean living on the underside of our social order in communities of mutuality, love, and endurance. Nonconformity means living in solidarity with the lowly: caring for the poor, loving enemies, renouncing retaliation, and overcoming evil forces by participating in God's goodness (Romans 12:9-21). Basically, nonconformity is a way of life that runs directly contrary to imperial logics while increasingly embodying the story of Jesus portrayed in Matthew, Mark, Luke, and John. Nonconformity, in the Pauline sense, is ultimately about conformity to the image of the Son. Since our discipleship takes precedence over our citizenship, our bodies, minds, and patterns of life must not become orchestrated by dominant culture.

This idea has huge implications for minorities who may find themselves lured and hypnotized by status and respect in America. Though it takes intellectual courage, renewed minds, and spiritual leading, it is crucial for minorities to realize that the way of Jesus is not consistent with the lure of status and respect. "Racial uplift" attained through playing by the rules of dominant society's patterns is *not* the new thing God is doing in Jesus Christ. Though American money, power, and respect are very enticing, full participation in dominant culture is also oppressive, perverse, and destructive.

The church must be a place where we take seriously the call to nonconformity in the way of Jesus. In doing so, we are drawn into further solidarity with the poor, oppressed, and "lowly," as Paul talked about. We refuse to participate in the death-dealing patterns of violence, but from below we experience God's goodness. Enjoying God's goodness in subversive, kingdom-manifesting communities of Christ provides the unexpected joy and blessing that is veiled from the awareness of Caesar. The value of encountering Jesus' presence in the world is still hidden from most. Yet once we find such a treasure, we will radically realign our entire lives to have it. We will renounce the cheap imitations of God's goodness found in societal respect and status. Instead, we will become transformed agents who subvert from below the lie of our current social order.

# 8

# RENOUNCING EVERY HIERARCHY

I never run into Native Americans where I live in Philadelphia. The shock of that statement eludes most of us. We are not baffled. We are not confused about how that could be. Our world and our identities will most likely not crumble and fall apart with that statement. Rather than needing to be put back together to reconsider our place on "American" soil, we move forward without as much of a hiccup.

The neighborhood I live in is on the border between the East Germantown and the Ogontz sections of Philadelphia, tucked right below the West Oak Lane neighborhood. Each of these communities are over 95 percent black. They are products of white flight. I regularly meet older white people who tell me that they use to live in neighborhoods around where I now live, but only when they were young. In Philadelphia, as the black population grew and inched northward, white people continually fled for purer (read: whiter) spaces that were yet "uncontaminated." So when I think about my neighborhood, my inclination is to think of it as black space. But of course the actual reality is much more complex and nuanced.

To understand the significance of my neighborhood's demographic, we must not only consider black experience or white
flight; we must also remember that the very foundations of this
country were formed by white people forcibly removing Native
Americans from their land. The story of white America is inextri-
cably bound to the continual breaking of treaties and covenants
with the Native American people and the near genocide that was
executed. We cannot understand America and its promise of pros-
perity for the tired and poor Europeans around the world except
by mulling over the ugliness of the Trail of Tears. Please understand: there is no understanding the present without knowing how
Native Americans have struggled in their own land just to exist.
And unfortunately, white Jesus was the symbol to which they were
told to conform. This meant letting their culture, stories, practices,
clothes, music, and wisdom die so that they could live into Anglo-
Saxon names, Western clothes, and white values.

I've struggled for the past couple of years to make sense of
the deep interconnectedness between black and Native American
experience in this land. Knowing deeply that such touchpoints
were definitely there, I still found it difficult to articulate how intimately our lives were bound to one another's because our experiences were so different.

Recently I was helped along the way when I attended an excel-
lent workshop led by Erica Littlewolf. Erica Littlewolf is from the
Northern Cheyenne tribe of southeastern Montana. During this
workshop, she and other facilitators guided participants through a
visual and active simulation of Native American history on Turtle
Island, the original name that many indigenous groups used to
describe the land that is now North America before its conquest
and colonization. Sitting on blankets that were spread out all over
the floor, we represented the indigenous peoples and tribes of the
land. We watched as people were forcibly removed from the land
and taken away (to represent the way people were killed off).

Toward the end of the session, when very few people were
left in the middle of the room on only a couple of blankets, we
were invited to process this experience together. Specifically,

we were invited to share about how we saw our own stories and identities fitting into this history that centralized Native American experience.

With each step through this simulated history, things started to click for me. This idea—that the experiences of different oppressed groups are interconnected—that had seemed so elusive was starting to make sense. Unfortunately, there were very few African Americans at the conference; I think I was the only black person in the room for this workshop. Nonetheless, I was excited to have the opportunity to flesh out what was going through my mind. I shared about the parallels and differences I saw between Native Americans and black Americans in this land. I connected the dots between how Native Americans had been forcibly removed from their own land and how African people at the same time had been forcibly brought to this land. The more that white people killed and displaced Native Americans, the more they sought to shackle and bring over black bodies. [The presence of the original hosts of the land constituted a threat to white identity and the sense of America as a "white country."] They had to be pushed out of sight onto reservations. Similarly, white society's need to forget the Native American people contrasts with its increasing surveillance over black bodies. The presence of subjugated black bodies treated like property was needed so that whiteness could mean superiority in the social hierarchy. More could be said on these similarities and differences—we could compare the one-drop rule and blood quantum laws, for example. But the point is that I had finally begun to comprehend the interconnectedness of black and Native American experience in this land.

Too many in the American church have perpetuated the myth that this land was built on Christian principles rather than on stolen land and stolen labor. Too many American Christians act as though this land justly belongs to white Anglo-Saxon people, and as the hosts of the land they could expect everyone to assimilate into their world. This false and dishonest history continues to erase four hundred years during which white Americans became a "den of robbers" (Jeremiah 7:11 NIV; Mark 11:17). Furthermore, it continues to suppress the important voices of Native American Christians, particularly those like Richard Twiss, who have refused to accept a whitened Jesus but have instead followed Jesus from the underside of the ongoing domination and colonization.[1]

I cannot understand my neighborhood without properly attending to the settler colonialism that my Native American sisters and brothers have suffered through. The church in America cannot conceive of what it means to live faithfully in the way of Jesus today if it continues to marginalize, silence, and forget Native Americans. In humility, and by grappling with the realities of white supremacy, the white church can repent from domination and recover its mode of life as strangers in the land. The church can turn away from its false belief that it is Christian destiny to dominate, control, and, when it desires, destroy everything and everyone in its way.

This chapter explores several aspects of oppression, in addition to white supremacy, that Christians and others need to understand. While I have tried to resist speaking of racism as merely the social and relational division between black people and white people, I have nonetheless written from my personal experience as a young black male. This book has been most attentive to white supremacy and antiblack ideology on the racialized ladder of our society. However, as Christians, we must not only challenge racial hierarchy (though in America that is particularly important). We must keep track of all forms of human-constructed hierarchies that exist in our communities. This is so that, as God's people, we can live more and more into the new humanity of Christ. Considering various people groups' experiences within *white supremacy* (racialized hierarchy) is vital, as is confronting *patriarchy* (gendered hierarchy) and *plutocracy* (classed hierarchy). Jesus reminds us that these ways of dominating others—which, as we shall see, often overlap and intersect—should be "not so with you" (Luke 22:26). As followers of Jesus, we are obligated to resist all types of lording over others.

---

1. Richard Twiss, *Rescuing the Gospel from the Cowboys: A Native American Expression of the Jesus Way* (Downers Grove, IL: InterVarsity Press, 2015).

## BEYOND BLACK AND WHITE

Conversations about racism frequently focus solely on the messy relationship between white and black people. White supremacy has been at the forefront of our attention in this book because it is the specific form in which our racialized, hierarchical society in the United States is ordered. However, no matter what racial category you have been squeezed into—black, white, Native American, Asian American, Arab American, Latino/a, or other—the reality is that everyone navigates this land in the present in light of the past four hundred years of white supremacy. No matter your place in this bigger story of conquest and slavery that produced—for some people—the possibility of the American dream, we are all participants in a still unfolding racialized story. We are all affected by white supremacy.

White supremacy has resulted in the colonizing and conquest of the Americas, forcing Native populations off their own land and onto reservations, oppressing early Chinese immigrant workers and excluding them from citizenship, sending Japanese immigrants into concentration camps during World War II, creating unjust and arbitrary immigration laws to keep Latin Americans from entering the country (as many European immigrants were allowed to do in the past), and taking prejudiced postures toward Muslim or Middle Eastern people. And that list doesn't even include the ongoing shift in the line of whiteness that has existed in this land, which meant that Irish and Italian immigrants were not initially considered white (meaning Anglo-Saxon Protestant) and were mistreated before eventually being adopted into the group as the majority's sociopolitical whims changed. White supremacy has been the common experience everyone has encountered.

For example, many Americans believe that the Asian American experience is proof that racism is no longer a prominent obstacle. Asian Americans' supposed "success," according to white dominant culture, suggests to them that other minority groups are delusional to think racism prohibits anyone. More critical and nuanced observations recognize the unique way that Asian Americans have been uniquely racialized as well.

Katelin Hansen, a white woman who created and writes for a blog on racial justice called *By Their Strange Fruit*, made some succinct observations concerning how Asian Americans often get set against black Americans by white dominant culture.[2] She illustrates this with a chart containing the stereotypes that white society has created to position the two minority groups as opposites. For example, blacks are stereotyped with terms like "ill-mannered, brainless, cool, athletic, lazy, bad parents, violent, break the law, high-school dropout, poor, succeed by preferences, fat, loud, bossy women," while stereotypes of Asians suggest they are "well-behaved, brainy, nerdy, bad at sports, hard-working, family-oriented, peaceful, make little trouble, Ivy-League University, well-to-do, succeed by merit, petite, quiet, submissive women." These stereotypes are substitutes for getting to know actual people who aren't essentialist characters. And not only that, Hansen maintains; these stereotypes actually work together to further normalize white standards as "balanced." Hansen explains, "Artificial polarization helps to pit people of color against each other, leading to division where we should have unity. The 'divide-and-conquer' strategy fuels modern racism. It also allows white folks to sit comfortably in the middle, further normalizing their culture relative to the 'extremes' around them."[3] Though many in white America stereotype Asian Americans as the "model minority group," the Asian American church has frequently not agreed with that vantage point. Asian American church leaders have expressed how they have been "misunderstood, misrepresented, and misjudged" by the mostly white evangelical church in America. For many Asian American Christian leaders, racism has continued to divide the church, and the pursuit of true reconciliation has not even begun.[4] Christian theologian Jonathan Tan

---

2. Katelin Hansen, "Dichotomy of Racialized Stereotypes," *By Their Strange Fruit* (blog), October 10, 2011, http://bytheirstrangefruit.blogspot.com/2011/10/dichotomy-of-racialized-stereotypes.html.

3. Ibid.

4. David Park, "An Open Letter from the Asian American Community to the Evangelical Church," *Next Gener.Asian Church* (blog), October 13, 2013, http://nextgenerasianchurch.com/2013/10/13/an-open-letter-to-the-evangelical-church-from-the-asian-american-community/.

asks some pointed questions that every white, dominant-culture church needs to begin taking seriously. He questions, "Why do Asian Americans, even the American-born third, fourth, and fifth generations of Mia Tuan's research, all find themselves regarded by the dominant white majority as foreigners who are regarded as 'not one of us,' but rather, as 'the Other'? Why is it that the dominant white majority calls for assimilation, and yet views Asian Americans as forever foreigners?"[5]

While Hispanic communities in the United States are extremely diverse and complex, the realities of white supremacy have certainly not skipped over these communities either. The most obvious and contentious concern today has centered on the unjust immigration laws that exist in our land. These laws, extending out of the ahistorical claim that white people have rights over the land, are to control and limit entry of people of color who are struggling economically or politically in other places. Many white Christians, while discussing immigration policy, seem to suggest that the issue is solely about what laws are on the books rather than the more important and Jesus-shaped questions: Does the law please God? Does the law reflect the inbreaking kingdom of Christ? As M. Daniel Carroll R., author of *Christians at the Border*, explains it,

> An appropriate response to the complicated situation in society will not come from detached, objective analysis, cost-benefit calculations, efficiency quotients, and cultural arguments. The decisions that are made and courses of action that are recommended should be commensurate with the life of Jesus—his actions, his teaching, his cross.[6]

Merely focusing on obeying the law is an intentionally short-sighted and irresponsible posture for disciples of Jesus. With that logic, a Christian who lived in 1850 would have had to fully endorse slavery. I believe that Augustine was right when he said, more than fifteen hundred years ago, that "an unjust law is no law at all."

5. Jonathan Y. Tan, *Introducing Asian American Theologies* (Maryknoll, NY: Orbis Books, 2008), 45.

6. M. Daniel Carroll R., *Christians at the Border: Immigration, the Church, and the Bible* (Grand Rapids, MI: Baker Academic, 2008), 139.

Both Jesus and the disciples modeled for us that we are called to break the law at times, so that we can live in alignment with God and love our neighbors faithfully. Besides, many tend to forget that Mexicans have a much deeper, longer, and more intimate relationship with the land on "our" side of the border than white Americans do. States like Texas, Arizona, and California, for example, were all Mexican territories at one time. A broader historical vision and biblically grounded perspective would flip the argument about land and belonging on its head.

More often than not, dominant-culture Christians describe undocumented immigrants as "illegal aliens" and "anchor babies," rather than as brothers and sisters in Christ. Many undocumented immigrants are Christians. Let us never forget that Jesus himself crossed boundaries constantly, including as a young boy when his family fled because of a lack of safety under Herod's regime. If Jesus' deep identification with immigrants crossing boundaries into new places for survival doesn't soften our hearts toward all immigrants, what will? The constant thread throughout the entire biblical narrative is to welcome the foreigner.

Also, many nonwhite Hispanic communities in urban centers are experiencing racialized challenges similar to those of black Americans. In my city of Philadelphia, many Puerto Rican youth are being targeted for nonviolent crimes that when committed by white people are often ignored or result in only a slap on the wrist. Young Latino youth also experience higher rates of convictions and harsher sentences than their white peers.

Finally, the gifts of Native American, Asian American, and Hispanic members in the church are often not valued. Too often our brothers and sisters are not even tokenized at Christian conferences or in Christian higher education; instead they are made completely invisible. Since Christianity among racialized minority groups is not in dangerous decline, as it is for most white American denominations, you would think that their communities would be tapped for insights and wisdom. Once we escape a limited, racialized framing of others, we might be able to also receive our brothers and sisters throughout the church as a gift.

The whole church desperately needs to renounce all forms of lording over others and all forms of centralizing white normativity. We need to make sure that the whole church can be seated around the table of God together as equals, where only Jesus is centralized and Lord over all.

## DISMANTLING MY SEXIST LENS

Attending my Christian college opened me up to the reality that racism wasn't the only type of oppression people regularly faced. The Christian community in which I grew up, though I love it dearly, didn't stretch me to think about the various ways that people experienced social hierarchy. I came to college thinking that, in general, I knew what I needed to learn in order to minister in the church. As a biblical studies major, I just needed a college education to deepen and further undergird my preexisting framework. I had no idea that, inside and outside of the classroom, my understanding would be shattered and put back together again.

Among many students who came from conservative evangelical communities, the biblical and religious studies department on campus had the reputation of leaning a bit to the left. But there was only one teacher whom I was actually warned about. There was only one professor I was told I should avoid if at all possible. This professor, according to many students, was a hard-core "feminist" who had an agenda against men. *Feminism* was not a word I heard much growing up. As my conservative peers let it roll off their tongues, you just knew it was a terrible thing. The last thing I needed was to sit with someone who had an agenda, I thought, someone who was going to impose her preconceived perspectives on me rather than sticking to what God actually taught us through Scripture.

Well, I couldn't really avoid taking this professor like most of my peers could, because I was a Bible major and needed to take certain courses in the department so that I would graduate in a timely fashion. Our professor's name was Dr. Reta Finger. Expecting a young, aggressive woman seeking to put all the male students in their place (because I had no context for knowing what feminists were like), I was surprised on my first day of class to encounter an older white Mennonite woman who spoke softly, stumbled in her speech, and was as gentle as they come. I wasn't fooled, though. I kept my radar on high alert, keeping watch for an unbiblical and unchristian feminist agenda.

Writing this more than a decade later, I only have generic memories of this class on the Gospels. But I do have one particular memory of when my professor slipped in her "agenda." We were studying Luke 7, exploring how a sinful woman had snuck into a house party of a Pharisee, anointed Jesus' feet with oil, and wiped them with her hair. It was a familiar story to me, but my professor brought this story to life for me during that class. I don't know if it was the Holy Spirit, the biblical background we had been studying, or my professor's insightful teaching—or a combination of the three—but suddenly I saw this story in a new way. I saw Jesus centralizing this woman while scolding a religious man who had clear social standing. Back and forth Jesus went, scolding this man for his neglect ("You did not . . . You did not . . . You did not . . .") and comparing it with her care (". . . but she . . . but she . . .") (Luke 7:44-46 NIV).

From that point forward, I began to see that Jesus was doing something radical in his society, challenging patriarchal expectations and limitations of women in a manner I had not known or been taught. This hard-core "feminist," with her supposed agenda, turned out to be someone who was merely trying to teach us the deeper implications of the good news of Jesus Christ, which included a radical new space for women to participate in community as equals when they were otherwise being lowered on the social hierarchy. Jesus, again and again, challenged the gendered hierarchy of his society. The violence of patriarchy had no place in God's kingdom come.

## DO YOU SEE THIS WOMAN?
Communities of racial minorities have often failed to see that while our entire community is experiencing oppression, oppression is being duplicated within our own groups in such a way that oppressed women find themselves on the bottom rungs of our internal hierarchical ladders. We are rightfully consumed by

the racism that affects all of us, but we must also be attentive
to how sexism continues without question. We challenge white
supremacy—but mostly how it affects black men, and not enough
in regard to vulnerable women's experiences in homes, churches,
and neighborhoods. We have willfully chosen not to see the patriarchy that persists as contrary to the way of Jesus.

Let's look more closely at the Luke 7 passage that challenged
me to see women, especially oppressed women, as God desires
us to. In Luke 7:36-50, Jesus is invited over to a Pharisee's house
for a dinner party. He has a space reserved at the table. His presence is welcomed. However, a woman realizes that Jesus will be at
this home and decides to crash the party unannounced. Upon her
arrival, the religious leader hosting the party only needs to glance
at her body to place her in one of his dehumanizing categories.
With only a look, he labels her. He only sees a "sinner" rather than
a woman made in the image of God, worthy of respect and dignity.
This stigmatization of her as a "sinful" woman—most likely what
we would call a "working girl"—was reason enough for many to
marginalize this woman in that society. Vulnerability is poured on
top of vulnerability for this woman who is seeking Jesus.

Nonetheless, the woman refuses to accept that limitation. She
refuses to be controlled by the categories into which the patriarchal system tries to force her. She takes bold action in faith. Unlike
the men, she recognizes Jesus' worth and anoints him with very
costly oil. The Pharisee, in his mind, believes he *knows* the essence
of this woman. For him, she is nothing more than a label: a "sinful
woman." She is a category rather than a human being.

This woman's seeking, anointing, and then clinging to Jesus
now binds both of them together in judgment before the Pharisee.
Jesus welcomes her into his presence rather than turning her away,
intentionally placing himself in solidarity with her.

Jesus could tell that this Pharisee had a vision problem. He
explored the world through the vantage point of male patriarchy
and female inferiority. He also gazed at people through a sim-
plistic binary that filtered people into either "clean" before God
or "unclean" sinner. In response, Jesus tells the Pharisee, Simon,

a story to stretch his framework, followed by a simple question: "Do you see this woman?"

Simon sees a sinner on the margins who could be disrespected, but Jesus sees a woman loved and created by God. Simon instantly judges this woman, as though he knows her essence. But Jesus flips the script and makes this marginalized woman the embodiment of God's inbreaking shalom. Jesus lifts up this woman as an example—a standard that this religious man has failed to meet. Jesus tells her to go and continue on in God's peace.

This story is not random or unexpected when considering the four gospel narratives. In what would have been a shockingly subversive story for its time, a vulnerable woman is affirmed and then centralized as a sign pointing to the arrival of the Messiah and life in God's kingdom. Throughout the gospel of Luke, Jesus is continually portrayed as caring for, standing in solidarity with, and often discipling women as worthy followers in a way that threatened the social order of his time and ours. The work of liberation, for Jesus, never skirted or missed women. His life focus made them part of his most vital priorities. Restoration, inclusion, healing, and deliverance of women from all forms of societal, spiritual, and physical oppression were continually a priority for Jesus' kingdom. This "sinful woman" whom Simon gazed at must be understood in light of this larger theme. Throughout his life, Jesus sought to bear witness to God's love for all women on the margins.

## BLACK WOMEN'S TROUBLES

On November 2, 2013, in the suburbs of Detroit, Renisha McBride got into a car accident and needed help. For a brief moment, McBride, a nineteen-year-old black woman, believed she had found a possible helping hand and a door of deliverance. In a mostly white suburban community outside Detroit, she stumbled up onto the porch of Theodore Wafer. As she knocked on the front door, Wafer opened the door and, through a locked screen door, shot her in the face. She died at the scene.

Having been wounded in a car accident in a strange neighborhood, McBride needed a good Samaritan. What kind of threat did she pose to this middle-aged white man? Did he just open the door, see a black woman, and immediately pull the trigger? Was he merely socialized by an American brand of racialized and gendered fear that didn't align with reality?

After the incident, many people sought to derail the conversation with character assaults aimed at this young black woman and to justify this violence by stigmatizing McBride as a "sinner." People wanted to talk about the fact that she had a high blood alcohol level. Certainly drinking and driving is irresponsible. No one has affirmed that initial decision of hers. Had she survived that night, she should have faced the appropriate consequences. But she did not survive that night, and it had nothing to do with her blood alcohol level. She survived a car crash, but she did not survive being a black woman in a white middle-class neighborhood.

Theodore Wafer gazed at Renisha McBride and saw someone dangerous, or at minimum someone unworthy of empathy. We should be paying attention to the fact that a white person's subconscious mind was socialized to respond in such a horrific way. People couldn't conceive of the possibility that our society is terribly sick from four hundred years of white supremacy and that it therefore routinely produces people who are sick. Such suggestions are never on the table as a necessary topic of discussion to move toward healing. Instead, this already marginal woman, who needed help in a moment of true need, was murdered, and then went through further marginalization after she was dead.

Even though Wafer was found guilty of murdering Renisha McBride that night, the court failed to do the harder work of exploring the subconscious decisions that create such irrational and fear-based behavior over and over again. Being a black woman in America comes with a lot of stigma, and our society has not come to terms with the different ways that race and gender overlap every day—sometimes with deadly consequences.

Other than tokenized people like Oprah Winfrey, women of color in our society are not given the same respect and dignity that most white women receive. In fact, news reports about Winfrey's experiences reveal that not even her great wealth can shield her from the stubborn and pervasive stigmas of race and gender. On one occasion, Winfrey was shopping at an expensive boutique in Switzerland. After expressing interest in a particular item, she was told by the store assistant it was too expensive and out of her price range. Yes, imagine Winfrey's surprise to be told that! Unbelievably, the store assistant actually refused to show her the item. Though Winfrey is wealthy enough that she probably could have just bought the entire boutique to make a point, she instead left immediately, deciding to not spend one dime at that establishment. Winfrey's financial peers are mostly white men, but her experiences are still differentiated because of gender and race.[7]

Now don't expend all of your sympathy on Oprah Winfrey; she is going to be okay. She still is a wealthy person living in comfort. Her wealth, celebrity, and tokenized status as America's favorite black woman provide her a much greater cushion than most people ever experience. The average black woman, however, is most likely living at the intersection of race, class, and gender oppression.

We have to assume that racialized, gendered, and classed biases constantly shape our everyday encounters. This is the case even when we are not conscious of it. It would be easy to make an example out of Wafer, as though he were an exception in America, as though he operated out of a different posture than most. But he merely swam in America's ocean of racialized and gendered vision. Renisha McBride was trying to navigate these waters as well. Unfortunately for her, being a black woman on that fateful night meant walking into a death-dealing space that was centuries in the making. It is only Jesus' deliverance that can provide victory from this horrific cycle of hierarchical oppression.

Anyone who gazes at a woman of color and assumes they can penetrate her being and categorize her essence must realize that Jesus stands in deep solidarity with oppressed women. No matter how much our society stigmatizes women of color, Jesus reminds us that they are made in the image of God. Jesus prophetically asks all of us, "Do you see this woman?"

Although we protest black men's wrongful deaths, too often dead black women get no rousing indignation from the African

---

7. Nick Thompson and Diana Magnay, "Oprah Winfrey Racism Row over Switzerland Shop Incident," CNN, August 11, 2013, http://www.cnn.com/2013/08/09/world/oprah-winfrey-racism-switzerland/index.html.

American community or from the larger society. Furthermore, black women have always been at the center of racial justice and liberation work in the church.

Who exactly were the ones filling up the pews at civil rights rallies in the church? Who made the flyers, on incredibly short notice, to notify the black community in Montgomery about the upcoming bus boycott? Who stood side by side with the men getting hosed in Birmingham? How about the important roles that women like Sojourner Truth, Ida B. Wells, Ella Baker, Diane Nash, Angela Davis, Michelle Alexander, and countless other black women have taken on for the benefit of the entire black community, especially on behalf of black men?

Isn't it time that we all not only acknowledge that courage but also reciprocate it by working to end the overlapping oppression of racism, sexism, and classism? Frequently, black women, and other women of color, are best positioned to understand the overlapping pressures of racial, class, and gender oppression because they creatively navigate these realities every day. While white supremacist patriarchy has often put the most visible pressure on black men, internally—that is, within the African American community, including the black church—black women frequently are treated without dignity on the underside of the social hierarchy.

## LORDING OVER OTHERS

We all have our pet oppressions and we like to stick to our lane. In contrast, many women around the world are constantly reminded that they have to creatively live at the intersection of being poor, female, and nonwhite. Many white men with varying social advantages frequently miss that their racial, gendered, and classed experience is not universal. Rather, it is particular and unique, which means other people's encounters in society result in varying outcomes. Similarly, individuals can be women or part of the LGBTQ community and experience discrimination in some areas of their lives but participate in and benefit from dominant culture, forgetting other social realities beyond their own. To be at the top of any social pecking order while universalizing your experience will typically result in ongoing oppressive hierarchical realities.

This is a problem that must be theologically defined as "lording over others," as Jesus discussed in Matthew 20:20-28:

> Then the mother of the sons of Zebedee came to him with her sons, and kneeling down she asked him for a favor. He said to her, "What do you want?" She replied, "Permit these two sons of mine to sit, one at your right hand and one at your left, in your kingdom." Jesus answered, "You don't know what you are asking! Are you able to drink the cup I am about to drink?" They said to him, "We are able." He told them, "You will drink my cup, but to sit at my right and at my left is not mine to give. Rather, it is for those for whom it has been prepared by my Father." Now when the other ten heard this, they were angry with the two brothers. But Jesus called them and said, "You know that the rulers of the Gentiles lord it over them, and those in high positions use their authority over them. It must not be this way among you! Instead whoever wants to be great among you must be your servant, and whoever wants to be first among you must be your slave—just as the Son of Man did not come to be served but to serve, and to give his life as a ransom for many."

I can picture this whole scenario. I can definitely picture a mom coming up to Jesus with her two sons, hoping that she can get her boys in the inner circle when Jesus becomes king. As they walked up to Jesus, Mama Zebedee probably spit on her hand to wipe food smudges off their faces. James and John were probably telling their mom that she was embarrassing them and that they could handle the task of asking Jesus themselves. Beyond my imagination, it is clear that Mama Zebedee is already convinced that Jesus is the Messiah and that he is going to be successful in overthrowing the Roman powers and restoring Israel. For this reason she seeks to do some politicking and maneuvering. That way, when Jesus "blows up," so to speak, her boys not only will be along for the ride but will actually be Jesus' right- and left-hand guys.

Jesus, however, responds by saying, "You do not know what you are asking! Are you able to drink the cup I am about to drink?" This response lets them know that they have no idea what they are actually asking for. Have you ever had a conversation with someone and realized partway through the discussion that you are talking about two completely different things? That's what is happening here. Jesus is trying to let them know that while they are both talking about the Messiah and his "enthronement," he and his disciples have completely different understandings of what that means.

Many Jews at that time hoped for a messiah who would come and violently overthrow the oppressive Romans, finally bringing Israel out of its state of exile even in their own land. Jesus, however, as described in the Gospels, understands that the Scriptures point to a Messiah who embodies and fulfills the role of the suffering servant. So when the Zebedee boys request to be on Jesus' left and right when they get to Jerusalem and Jesus is enthroned, in reality Jesus' left and right will be occupied by two other men. On crosses.

After that exchange, the other ten disciples are angry with the brothers. Why? My guess is that they are mad because they didn't think of it first, not because they are disgusted by the brothers' complete failure to envision what God was up to. The disciples have been raised in a society in which their people have been on the bottom side of the social hierarchy for generations. Most likely, as is the case for most oppressed people, they experience a compli- cated hatred mixed with envy toward those who reign over them. They may despise the Romans and want to rid themselves of their overbearing imperial presence, but they also probably covet their lifestyle and the wealth flaunted in their faces. People often uncon- sciously imitate and shape their ambitions after those in power at the top of the social hierarchy. I'm sure that was the scenario for all of these disciples.

So Jesus once again responds to his disciples, gathering them together for another huddle. This time he says to them, "You know that the rulers of the Gentiles lord it over them, and those in high positions use their authority over them" (Matthew 20:25). Jesus isn't blind to the social hierarchy in his society. He names and unveils the social ladder upon which the Roman Empire was built. And in doing so he pulls back the curtain on their desires. Jesus' disciples want to live just like these rulers who lord over others.

But Jesus says, "It must not be this way among you!" (Matthew 20:26). Jesus does not make lording over others an option for his disciples. Unfortunately, most churchgoers today don't appear to know that. People have found a way to call themselves Christian, which means to be Jesus-shaped, and still chase after power without thinking twice about it. We disregard Jesus' teaching on power and how we ought not to use it to dominate others. Our practice, though, doesn't change the fact: Jesus says that it must not be so!

Lording over others in our context normally occurs at the intersection of racialized, gendered, and economic oppression. Understanding how the experiences of various oppressed people groups are intertwined is essential in all the antiracist work we do. Our antiracism work will be limited if we don't take account of these various facets of domination. Therefore, we must understand that all of life is always racialized and gendered. In unison, the church must commit to ending all oppression. The church must become the people who renounce lording over others in all manners, whether white supremacy, patriarchy, or economic domination. Instead, we must turn to the way of Jesus as the pathway to new life.

## THE MYTH OF THE SUPERIOR WHITE MALE FIGURE

Despite all the Christian rhetoric, our society in America has never been configured around the way of Jesus Christ. The centralized figure in our culture has not been the crucified and risen Lord. The one our lives revolve around is not the image of the Son. The body to which everyone else has had to align and conform has been the white, wealthy, Western male image. Assumed to be balanced, objective, measured, and well-reasoned, this elite white male image has been sitting at the top of the social hierarchy, and it has organized life for all of us. White men themselves do not even live up to the myth, but the constructed image nonetheless has justified white men's superiority to other people groups and women for centuries.

Reading history closely illuminates the myth of the white male figure that has justified white supremacy, patriarchy, and plutocracy around the globe. Whether it be Constantine in the fourth century, Christopher Columbus in the fifteenth century, or Thomas Jefferson in the eighteenth century, Western men of power and means have been lifted up as heroes and as ideal human beings. The myth, however, strangely covered up or overlooked all of their horrific violence: Constantine was a violent, imperial conqueror; Columbus was a pillager of land and resources; and Jefferson was a slaveholder and rapist. In more subtle ways, this pattern continues today.

I was once invited to offer feedback to the staff of a Christian organization planning a national Christian conference. The leaders, who were both white men, believed I might be able to assist them in creating a more racially diverse event. I offered various suggestions, but the two most critical things I emphasized were that they needed to break up their all-white, male decision-making group. That no racial minorities or women were part of the planning for this event seemed an obvious problem, with a simple fix. Second, they had designed the event by centralizing three white men as the speakers before considering whether there might be people of color better suited to speak on those topics. It seemed obvious to me that the planners should not tokenize people of color and women by making them afterthoughts—sprinkles around the all-vanilla dessert, which was clearly the central focus.

Various disagreements grew out of those conversations. In the end, a small number of people of color were added—after and around the initial white men who remained in place. A couple of white women spoke from the front. And while African American males were greatly underrepresented as well, what was even more problematic for me was that not one woman of color was asked to participate in the entire conference. Not from the stage or in any workshop. It was clearly much more troubling to me than it was to these planners, who probably thought they were merely putting on a helpful Christian conference. They couldn't see how white and male hierarchical power was being exercised through exclusivity. They interpreted their own actions through a lens of innocence throughout most of the process. They initially couldn't conceive that they were playing a familiar role in American history.

I deeply believe that they had good intentions in creating their conference and that they certainly didn't plan to marginalize, tokenize, or totally make invisible racial minorities or women. Yet the good intentions of people in power coupled with ignorance provide no hopeful path forward in matters of exclusion and white male centrality. No matter how things unfolded, if my friends were not willing to break free of the script of the mythic white male's normative position—always objective and unbiased, while occupying the central place of power—then their projects were bound to have flaws. Until dominance is radically reconfigured toward a flattened hierarchy, the status quo remains.

The myth of white male superiority in America is the standard against which all people (including but not limited to women, people of color, and even poor whites) are measured. It runs at the heart of the American experiment. We know that when Thomas Jefferson penned that it was "self-evident" that all men were created equal, he only had in mind white, landowning men. The image of manhood created equally, for Jefferson, was always projected in his imagination as a white man of means. For that reason he could continue holding enslaved Africans and ponder sending them back to Africa as a long-term solution. There was no long-term place for black bodies in the United States outside of servitude, from his perspective.

The centrality of a Western, wealthy, powerful white body was so great that Jesus' image and meaning had to go through necessary conversions. Yes, Jesus, in the hands of Western society, had to be refashioned into a white male figure, and the image remains on the walls of churches and homes even today. Clearly the poor Jewish Messiah living under Roman domination wasn't sufficient to be Lord over all creation. For four hundred years in this land, white elite men have been lord. Many poor whites have played along, though rarely did they receive much from the social arrangement other than making dark bodies into scapegoats and receiving a slight psychological satisfaction that they weren't at the very bottom of the social ladder. The myth of the superior white male figure stands at the center of our society, and it does for most of the American church as well.

When people want to learn about God revealed in Jesus Christ, there stands the mythic white male figure. Some white male theologians and preachers frequently make Jesus sound more like Uncle Sam than the nonviolent, Jewish revolutionary described in the gospel narratives. With a pseudowhite male Jesus let loose in the church, the boundaries of acceptable theological reflection have neatly aligned with powerful, elite American male interests. The myth of the white male figure has quietly supervised most Christian conversations, often shaping the discourse and theological reflections of nonwhite followers of Jesus.

Though it is undisputed that Western forms of Christianity have participated in some of the most atrocious and violent acts within church history, the mythic white male figure claims clarity and objectivity in asserting who is in or out of bounds. This is why the church of power has been violently preoccupied with labeling people as heretics and heathens. It seeks to maintain clear political control over the boundaries of the church.

My professor in seminary, John Franke, used helpful language in the classroom to discuss the role white theologians and preachers have played in theological discourse in the church. According to him, white male theologians have often seen themselves as objective and neutral overseers of the Christian tradition. They function as "theological referees" for everyone else, while imagining their position as neutral and unbiased in the center of all the action. Believed to be "fair and balanced" and merely passing on the "classical" teachings of Christ, white men of means in the church label everyone else who doesn't fit into their mode of thought. Others do "black theology," "Latin American theology," "womanist theology," or "peace theology." White men, however, seen as universal and objective—as though they hover over culture rather than participate in it—merely do "theology." No label or descriptor is necessary. Everyone else is shaped by their context and experience, but white men apparently are not. The experience of racism or poverty or gender discrimination is assumed to make others subjective and therefore ill-equipped to teach the pure, unadulterated Word of God.

What seems to be missing in this equation is that white men have a social context too. Why wouldn't the posture of relative wealth, the practice of racial dominance, and patriarchy result in theologies being domesticated and adjusted to permit or justify such social realities? The myth of the elite white male figure has blinded us to the limitations of those who have charged themselves with protecting the tradition for everyone else. Those who claim that Jesus pointed toward a new path and that the poor and oppressed frequently understand this new path best—these folks are somehow always seen as deviating from the truth. But whose account lines up most with what Jesus himself taught?

Criticizing the social construction of white identity is often seen as stepping out of bounds of faithful Christian witness. Speaking from a position of power, the supposedly superior white male figure makes those labels stick and further stigmatizes marginalized Christian groups. The mythic white male figure appears apolitical, but in actuality his strategic power moves reaffirm hegemony and shut out dissenting voices. Many people groups, far beyond those defined by racial categories, have experienced such marginalization.

As long as the white male figure grounded in superiority, in all its mythic and legendary glory, stands at the center, the actual Jewish Messiah, who is Lord over heaven and earth and who holds all things together, will not be recognized for his centrality and preeminence. The manipulation to make Jesus look like, think like, and act in congruence with the myth of the white male figure is *not* the Jesus found in Matthew, Mark, Luke, and John. It is an imposter. We might go as far as to say that it is an antichrist.

The living and resurrected one did not, and still does not, incarnate into the life and disposition of the oppressor. Rather, Jesus' way is found in his humble birth, subversive teachings, radical life, and his state-sanctioned execution by the authorities of the establishment, which found him to be a threat to the status quo. Claiming the center stage, just like Pharaoh and Caesar did in their time, has always been a blasphemous overreach that actually places oneself on the margins of God's reign. The church must resolutely pursue new life, new humanity, and new creation where Jesus is at the center rather than on the outside, knocking, and waiting to get in.

## JESUS, BE THE CENTER

We must reorient our lives to make the true Jesus the center of our lives. The church must decentralize the white male figure's pre-eminence. Despite how people often hear this language in dominant culture, decentralizing white male prestige is not an attack on white men. At its heart, it is the opposite: it is a humanizing project.

Lording over others demands that people be apathetic to the racialized other. It means gazing on an individual with bias or contempt and seeing something other than someone God found to be worthy to lay down God's own life for. When one succumbs to playing into the role of the white male image, that person embodies something other than what our Creator desired of humanity—something predator-like that is puppeted by the elemental forces of this world and the dominion of Satan. It is precisely in our attempts to seize God's position that things begin to quickly fall apart.

Decentralizing the white male figure's blasphemous godlike position is necessary so that people can be restored to the image of God. Realizing this new humanity in Christ will mean that those that have become accustomed to standing at the center must now step off the table as the social, political, and theological referees lording over everyone else. Instead, *everyone* is invited to sit around the table as equals. There is so much more we can learn about God in Christ Jesus when we dialogue together on level terms. The hierarchy has been flattened, and only Jesus is preeminent. No longer controlled by the logic of white male centrality in the church, people are liberated to embrace God's beloved community as equals in Christ (Galatians 3:28).

Christian communities that want to undo racism must renounce all hierarchies. Christians must realize that our whole society is affected by white supremacy and antiblack racism—and that includes Hispanic, Asian, and African immigrants as well as long-time citizens. Black Americans must recognize the ways that other groups experience concrete oppression and struggle alongside them as well. And we all must keep track of racism, sexism, and classism. Ultimately, it is the Jesus who identified with and sought to restore the Samaritans, poor people, and vulnerable women who compels us to renounce these hierarchies in our everyday Christian labors of love.

In following Jesus and centralizing him in the church, God's people will find an alternative response to racialized hierarchy and white supremacy in our society. Right under the noses of all those lording over others is a space created for the church of Jesus Christ. And from that Jesus-shaped solidarity, a prophetic movement that is a light to the corners of our world can begin. Jesus-shaped communities should be the visible communities where lording over others is renounced, in all its forms, whether in regard to racial, gendered, or classed hierarchy. Only Jesus is Lord.

So how can we practically embody this confession, day to day? How can we acknowledge with our lives that Jesus is Lord?

# 9

# WHERE DO WE GO FROM HERE?

**W**e as Christians must follow Jesus and courageously break allegiances with white supremacist, classed, and patriarchal hierarchies, joining in solidarity with the stigmatized: whether a black man being labeled as a thug as a justification for denying his human dignity; a young Hispanic woman being treated as a nonhuman because of her lack of documentation; a Muslim being harassed for her faith; or a queer teen facing bullying in school. Jesus' way was never a path toward hierarchical coercion. We must learn to see a world Jesus has begun to flip right-side up so that those most despised as last and least valued are now first and most esteemed. Jesus gave priority to Samaritans, vulnerable women, the poor, and other social outcasts of his day, and gave them prime seats in God's kingdom. We need to engage in faithful embodied practices and Christian disciplines that help us take the first steps out of the cycles of oppression and toward the shalom of Christ.

## SEVEN JESUS-SHAPED PRACTICES FOR THE ANTIRACIST CHURCH

So let's get concrete about what this might look like. I would like to suggest seven embodied practices, or disciplines, to get folks going on the journey. These are constructed from my own theological and ethical faith journey, lessons I've gleaned from personal experience, and the wisdom of others I respect. I believe that these things need to become the norm for the church if we are going to faithfully live in racialized America. These practices will not only address the cultural gap of difference but also challenge us to concretely follow Jesus in a way that undermines our racialized and hierarchical society. They will help us disentangle our everyday lived faith from unconscious racialized socialization and will move us toward becoming truly reconciled communities capable of resisting racial violence and oppression.

These practices do not need to be followed in some sort of chronological order. They are not steps to follow or some process one must move through one at a time. Rather, they are embodied spiritual practices that one can begin at any point. Most likely, multiple practices will need to happen simultaneously. And doing one ought to inevitably put you at the doorstep of the others.

### Share life together

Ephesians 2 reminds us that the reconciliation Jesus inaugurated broke down the walls of hostility between Jews and Gentiles so that, through the cross of Jesus, such barriers could be overcome. Truly sharing life together while gathered in the presence of the stigmatized, crucified, and now resurrected Messiah is now possible.

What I am gesturing toward isn't the idea of merely attending the same church service as people from another racial group. It's something much grander than that. The practice of sharing life together has everything to do with no longer allowing the racial hierarchy to pattern our social lives, manage our geographic movements, shape identities of superiority and inferiority, or interpret one another through white supremacist and antiblack gazes. We are free to follow Jesus into forbidden spaces we were socialized to avoid, spaces in which we previously believed we didn't belong. Sharing life together means intimately identifying with people who carry the stigma of varying racial meanings in their actual bodies. Most practically, this can be expressed in regularly sharing life together around the table, as well as in Christian communal disciplines like reading and interpreting Scripture and praying together. The table—and I specifically mean sharing meals together—offers an opportunity to practice hospitality and intimacy that renounce racial hierarchy and racialized social patterns.

### Practice solidarity in the struggle

Jesus proclaimed, "The Spirit of the Lord is upon me, because he has anointed me to proclaim good news to the poor" (Luke 4:18). And guess what? That is exactly what Jesus went out and did. He went out liberating those oppressed physically, socially, and spiritually. He identified with the poor and the hungry and invited them to participate in a kingdom of justice and peace in which the most vulnerable are no longer neglected. He joined in their lives and experienced their struggles. Jesus knew what it was like to have a cousin executed by the powers that be. He personally understood the vulnerable feeling of being picked up at night, put through an unfair trial, and executed by the authorities without anyone to champion his cause.

As we follow Jesus into the world, we must join with racially oppressed communities. We must so deeply identify with them that their struggle becomes our struggle. Christians do not merely watch as distanced spectators. We are dropped right into the conflicts of the world, and with Jesus we march right toward confrontation with our own Jerusalem-like establishments, where prophets are killed and power is concentrated.

Practically then, for Christians not yet engaged in justice work, I suggest that you explore what is already happening in your region rather than trying to start something new. It is too easy to try to be saviors when in reality we are just allowing our egos to operate. We need to come alongside good people already doing good work. Only very rarely is it the case that no one in the community is already doing the work. If there is a need not being addressed at all, or one that is too great for one group to address, then go forward, but still under the wisdom and accountability of those who are directly affected by the social injustice. Regardless, you should take inventory of what is already happening before you make a move. What local or regional churches or organizations are already struggling for racial justice? Do your research, and then humbly join in and be willing to be led.

Solidarity requires that socially advantaged people realize that their life in this racialized society requires them to use their bodies as a living sacrifice. In joining in the struggle and encountering the presence of Jesus in new and unimagined ways, people will be amazed at how their fractured relationships with God, others, and themselves are reconciled. Followers of Jesus are both the oppressed and those who come alongside oppressed people, link arms with one another, and walk in solidarity while confronting the injustice of society in a manner that is faithful to the way of Jesus.

### See the world from below

The third embodied practice is seeing the world from below. It's interesting that in Luke 10:21-22, Jesus praises the little ones who see things that the wise and learned will never see. Paul, while speaking to the Corinthians, reminds us that God has chosen the weak and vulnerable to shame the strong and powerful (1 Corinthians 1:27-28). In fact, the entire biblical narrative reveals a God who chooses to move and work most forcefully in the cracks, margins, and edges of society. It is to the poor, the foreigners, the widows, and the rejected that God's kingdom appears. We learn from that vantage point that it is not Pharaoh, nor Nebuchadnezzar, nor Caesar, nor the president, nor wealthy men like Donald Trump who move history along.

Even in the church, we have been tempted to keep our eyes fixed on the powerful. No, it is the crucified Christ—the one crushed by worldly power—through whom we understand that God's mission takes place most decisively on the axis of vulnerability. We would be wise, then, to turn toward Jesus and join him in the company of the oppressed.

Practically, I suggest that Christians from dominant culture change their reading habits so that those on the margins become the main stage. In the church, I suggest intentional group circles that are racially diverse, where stories can be shared and received.

Maybe using a book about racism or reconciliation as a tool to facilitate the conversation would help.

People need to put their bodies in places where they are going to slowly learn to see things that they never would otherwise. The secret that followers of Jesus find along the journey is that the view from below, rather than above, offers a better position from which to see what God is up to. Therefore, I suggest learning to not trust your own intuitions, which have been shaped by socialization in racially hierarchical and segregated white spaces.

### Subvert racial hierarchy in the church

Racial hierarchy needs subverting. It needs subverting from below, at the grassroots level. The powers that be lord over others, but Jesus and his kingdom create the new world right under the nose of the social hierarchy. Just as Jesus, in Luke 13:31-35, defied Herod and then continued on with the work of liberating healing and justice-filled shalom, so too must Christians subvert every way that our society's racial hierarchy is allowed to exist. This subversion must happen first and foremost in the church. Once again, in refusing to be a puppet of racial socialization, the church must undermine any project that concentrates white power over others or that normalizes white values, experience, and perspectives as the objective and universally right way. Instead, the church must subversively embrace the new humanity and the diverse gifts and varied perspectives that exist within it. It must intentionally privilege the voices and perspectives of those in society who are most neglected, forgotten, ignored, and silenced. The community that has visibly flipped things upside down will not define its life by the standards and expectations of dominant culture. Risking being labeled foolish or inefficient, the subversive community, under the lordship of Jesus, will patiently dialogue in community, believing that God's Spirit can speak through someone without a high school diploma as clearly as through someone with a PhD.

Practically, this subversive kingdom life means that everything is up for critique and change. It means that the community's life must yield itself to the concerns of those historically excluded. It means that things like job descriptions, church food and meal choices, book selections, curriculum structures, money allocation, meeting times, and the composition of decision-making groups like the church board must be radically reconfigured. These things must become signposts of faithfulness to the God who sustains all of life, and whom every tribe, nation, and tongue will one day worship.

## Soak in Scripture and the Spirit for renewed social imagination

We must also develop Scripture-soaked social imaginations. The biblical narrative's subversive and prophetic window into our own world has been lost on too many Christians, who have read Israel's texts as though they confirmed hierarchy, power, and empire. The West has read Scripture through a Eurocentric vantage point of white superiority. Rather than allowing Scripture to be read against conquest, colonization, and white supremacy, in some strange way Christians have manipulated the Bible's story to confirm those things and marginalize Christ's centrality in the narrative.

When we read Scripture through the lens of Jesus, as God's Messiah and suffering servant, Scripture is unlocked. Jesus, who was vindicated in and victorious over the cross, reveals that God has consistently chosen the socially weak and vulnerable to shame the mighty and powerful. Throughout Scripture, God takes sides. God is not neutral in the midst of human suffering and oppression. It is not by accident that the divine name of Yahweh was revealed while God delivered the Israelites from the slavery and oppression of the Egyptians.

Going forward, this holy and hallowed name would forever be remembered and celebrated as intimately intertwined with God's deliverance for this oppressed people, who had been called out into covenant relationship with God. They were to be a light to the nations, extending and embodying God's justice in the world. And when they lost sight of that and got caught up in monarchies and injustice toward others, God sent the prophets, who condemned the injustice and idolatry that deviated them from their calling as God's suffering servants. Whether written under the thumb of Egypt, Babylon, Assyria, or Rome, Scripture narrates that God worked on the underside of dominance through weakness to express divine power and transformation. Jesus' birth, life, death, and resurrection unveil him as God's Messiah who brings down thrones, sends the rich away empty-handed, and fills the hungry and poor with good things. From the edges of life, Jesus inaugurates a kingdom of justice and peace.

The church in the West has rarely made sense of this powerful story because we have been too busy dissecting it for intellectual purposes. If we would dare to yield ourselves, through the Spirit while in community with marginalized people, to reading, hearing, and living out this story, we would see afresh and with kingdom insight. Never has it been more important to drench ourselves in the story of Scripture, which will renew our minds and empower us to resist the currents of racial conformity in our world.

Of course, there is no transformation through the reading of Scripture without also yielding to the Holy Spirit in the world. The Holy Spirit is active and alive in our world. The Holy Spirit is guiding the church toward all truth. And the Holy Spirit is subversive, blowing here and there as it wills. Despite the suffering and violence we see all around us, God has not abandoned us. God's Spirit is at work transforming, restoring, liberating, and empowering people to hold on. Wherever Jesus' delivering presence is encountered, there is God's Spirit. When communities are following and being formed after Jesus, there is God's Spirit. When people are being formed after the image of the Son, sharing in both the suffering and resurrection of Christ in the world, there is God's Spirit. God's Spirit gives the church the courage to resist and stand strong. When we need the right words to speak before authorities and powers as we testify to the truth of our Lord and the kingdom of God, the Spirit gives us such words. The Spirit binds the church together. Baptized into the Spirit, we are knitted together as one body. And the evidence of lives yielded to the Spirit and soaked in Scripture will always be lives that are Jesus-shaped.

### Seek first the kingdom of God

As a Christian discipline, we must learn, with anticipation, to seek first the kingdom of God. The kingdom of God is like hidden treasure in a field that someone finds and that prompts them to sell all they have so that they can purchase that field (Matthew 13:44). It is worth every ounce of sweat you spend searching for it. When you find it, you will realign your whole life according to that discovery.

For this reason we must never forget to seek first, before anything else, God's kingdom. Jesus warned his listeners that they needed to repent (which means to change one's life), because the kingdom of God was quickly approaching. He often told them that the kingdom was near or, at times, already in their midst. The future reality has sneaked into our present concrete world, even though we live within the decay of this old and sinful age. Ultimately, Jesus' prayer, which ought to shape our own prayers, centered God's kingdom on earth, so that God's will would be done here as it already is being done in heaven. Studying the gospel narratives reveals a strong correlation linking the good news of God's kingdom, God's peace and shalom, and God's righteousness and justice. The kingdom of God has come and still is coming, setting things right according to God's new creation. God's kingdom is good news for those living in seemingly hopeless circumstances.

Jesus rebooted humanity and creation. Of course, the world doesn't look like that is so yet, given all of its social hierarchies and ongoing violence. At the center of the kingdom of God is Jesus. Origen, one of the most important and influential early Christian theologians, called Jesus *autobasileia*, which basically means "self-kingdom." Jesus, then, is the seed of the kingdom of God by himself, embodying and revealing what is to come.

Now, to be clear: the kingdom of God is not automatic nor is it ritually manifested. The church isn't the kingdom of God just because we call ourselves Christian, or because we partake in sacraments, or because someone preaches on Sunday, or because we affirm and hold to a particular set of confessions. The church is the kingdom of God when and only when Jesus is present in a community that is taking on his form and way in the world. When our community begins to mirror the poor in spirit, those who mourn, the meek, those who hunger and thirst for righteousness, the merciful, the pure in heart, the peacemakers, and those persecuted for righteousness, then it is there the kingdom of God has become visible and real in our world.

Jesus' ministry and the parables he told about the kingdom of God have not been taken seriously enough. We have too easily aligned our lives to the way of America, because its lifestyles are taken for granted as right and true. We have too often been distracted by the American dream, pursuing life, liberty, and the pursuit of happiness instead of God's reign on earth. However, one day we will find that it is not America but the kingdom of God that is "the beautiful." The church will joyfully sell all the ugliness of racialized hierarchy, sexist patriarchy, and selfish classism when we find the true treasure in the field.

### Engage in self-examination

Finally, we have a lot of self-examination work to do if we are going to be the called-out people gathered around Jesus and then scattered and sent back into our society. Christians are supposed to reserve our sharpest criticism for ourselves. Yet we have spent so much time criticizing our society for what we perceive to be wrong while walking around with an attitude of self-righteousness. This, of course, seems hypocritical to non-Christians, who are often more aware of the skeletons in our closets than we are conscious of them ourselves.

If we are to be a church that is salt and light, showing our good deeds before others as Jesus called us to do, then our first task is to take the log out of our own eye and stop fussing over the specks that we find in others' eyes. Each of us must engage in some soul-searching and self-examination. No one in America is untouched by the currents of racial bias and white supremacy. I know I am not outside of it, though I wish I were. Considering all that has gone on in our country, we are delusional if we think that we have not at least partially caught the American racialized disease of white supremacy and antiblack bias. Of course we have. Now is not the time to fall into denial.

Thankfully, we have the call to come before Jesus' table and to examine ourselves before the body of Christ (which means all of its collective members). Just as the Corinthian believers found their community to be divided because of the economic hierarchy taking precedence in their lives, we must also look clearly and critically at our communities to name our divisions. We must take seriously our own racialized identity and socialization. This is particularly hard for white Christians to do, because it is the very thing many have often been taught not to do. The truth is that everyone in America has a racial identity that has been socialized from living here. The greatest danger is when we are unaware or in denial of that socialization.

Practically speaking, white Christians especially need to learn about the development of race and white identity in America. Understand how it works so you aren't its puppet. Don't be afraid to talk about racism in spaces that will challenge and transform how you think. Read and reflect on who you are and how you have come to understand yourself within our racialized society. Resist normalizing your own experience, but instead seek to explore and expose your own inconsistencies. Most of all, as people surrendered to the Holy Spirit, we must all ask God to reveal those areas in our lives that need God's transformative work. All of us need this kind of self-examination and Spirit-filled transformation in our lives.

## BEYOND SIMPLISTIC HOPES FOR THE "MULTIETHNIC CHURCH"

Some people, with great excitement, have put lots of hope for a better future within our racialized society into the existence of the "multiethnic church." I'm not so optimistic. For one, such churches are still extremely rare, because most people flock toward racial segregation. Also, having been part of such a community for a few years, I know the complexities of multicultural and multiethnic churches. Some people desire merely to attend a diverse service for an hour or two on Sunday morning, while their lives the rest of the week are just as racialized as everyone else's. Baylor University released a recent study suggesting that black people attending a multiethnic church were more likely to hold views that resemble the perspectives of most white people in society than other black people.[1] My observation is that most multiethnic churches are normed by white, dominant-culture sensibilities, even when diversity is being reflected on the stage. And it is a real struggle for communities to break from that stronghold.

That said, I've seen churches in Harrisburg and Philadelphia be better than that—but only when we risked digging deeper below the surface stuff. After college graduation, during my time as the youth pastor of Harrisburg Brethren in Christ Church, a multiracial church in the city, I began my long journey of groping for a more hopeful way than what I had seen in other churches.

During my time in the Harrisburg congregation, I was part of a pocket of people within the larger structure of the organized church who truly did life together. We were challenged and stretched by one another and sought another way of following Jesus. This included speaking truth to power and seeking for a more just way. I know we were not the only pocket within that community exploring what it meant to truly be immersed into the Jesus story. The presence of a multicultural church, merely as an institution or service, can oversell the amount of transformation that is happening. But that same institution has the opportunity to create intentional spaces where racism is discussed and studied, and where hierarchies are dismantled.

Since coming back to Philadelphia to get my MDiv and to work on my doctorate, I have had the pleasure of connecting with a group of Christian leaders every month. We dwell in the Word together, pray for one another, support the various projects and ministries each of us are involved in, and collaborate on justice and mercy initiatives. This group created a construction company that intentionally employs folks reentering our neighborhoods after serving time in prison, which is in response to a great need in most poor black and brown communities. We have one church that was planted with a primary focus of ministering to those in prison and to those who have been released from prison, journeying with them as they seek the difficult road of restoration in

1. "Racial Attitudes of Blacks in Multiracial Congregations Resemble Those of Whites, Study Finds," Baylor University Media Communications, August 17, 2015, http://www.baylor.edu/mediacommunications/news.php?action=story&story=159118.

Philadelphia. Another leader and her church work closely with a religious organization that seeks to address systemic injustice in our city's structures by organizing leaders to bear prophetic witness on a variety of issues. They've called for an increase in minimum wage for the working class, a new paradigm for public education, and transformation and accountability in our judicial system. I've been pleased to see our various churches get out and march with other groups in our city so that the church's presence and full identification with the least of these in Philadelphia is known and heard.

Another church in our network, based in South Philadelphia, is composed of several immigrant groups. Many of their church members and neighbors in the community are undocumented. Nonwhite immigrants have been especially vulnerable because of immigration laws. So this church community boldly provides sanctuary for people our country would seek to reject. They know that their calling as the church is always to welcome the foreigner in their midst (Leviticus 19:34; Deuteronomy 10:19). Other churches are doing economic and community development, especially empowering youth and adults in their neighborhoods. Others are welcoming people into community and belonging who are unchurched or have felt alienated in the body of Christ.

Collectively, rather than through each individual leader or individual Christian community, I see God transforming the church. We are not seeking to merely be the church *for* the poor and oppressed; as we work toward a more Jesus-shaped way of Christian community, we hope to be the church *of* the poor and oppressed.

## NOT THE END OF THE TROUBLED STORY

I love being me. I love my body. I love the people who I have had the pleasure of journeying with. I've loved reflecting on the meaning of life, with all its joys and pains, in my dark body, within the only land I know as home.

Yet *home* is such a conflicted word to describe what America is to me. It has fashioned me in a deep and intimate way, but I am perpetually caught somewhere between belonging and alienation.

And while that sense of never fully belonging may very well be an appropriate response to the call to follow Jesus, it ought not to be subjected on anyone merely because he or she is of African descent. Every day when I wake up, I know I might encounter anything within the spectrum from distrust to death. I am caught, without any choice, within the long story of white supremacy. Making sense of the insensible is a necessary task for keeping sane in this country. Remembering the nonsense of white supremacy can be summed up in the acknowledgment that I've seen so much trouble.

Those who know me well, beyond the "public theology" I engage in, know that I am fairly skeptical about America's potential to become a global leader for justice and peace. We have yet to admit that everything that happens in the present is merely the unfolding of America's birth: stolen land and conquest, genocide of Native Americans, stolen labor from African people, and the development of a dehumanizing antiblack ideology. The very myths that have been designed to cover up this troubled story have at times inspired courageous individuals to hope for a better America.

But I am doubtful that America will ever live up to its myths. I don't anticipate real transformational justice to flow from government policies (though tweaks and reform shouldn't be dismissed as nothing), or from wealthy people engaged in philanthropy (though charitable giving can bring temporary relief), or from our favorite celebrities (though some might inspire us). We have spent too much time looking in the wrong direction.

I do think, however, that communities within the story of America can do better. In response to all of this trouble that I've seen—and maybe you have seen it too—our hope must turn toward communities living in the presence of Jesus within the cracks and holes of the world. The American church has mostly preoccupied itself with an idolatrous love of power and wealth. We have sought, over and over again, to grasp and seize hold of power. We have hoped that presidents would let justice roll down like waters, and we have had faith that wealthy business owners would let righteousness flow like ever-flowing streams (Amos 5:24).

I have been persuaded that the church's power is different from our society's power, and it is released by God at the axis of human vulnerability. There the church can be salt and light for the world—not because it is so virtuous in and of itself, but because it is following Jesus and yielding to the Spirit's presence. Said another way, my hope is that change can happen in America because God has always chosen the most vulnerable and oppressed to shame the strong. And that story isn't finished being told yet.

There is urgency to this good news. If this book has failed, it has probably failed to communicate the weightiness of the moment. Beyond changing how we view racism, we must live differently. We must be transformed. And we must be transformed not only for our own sake but because, every day, people are dying. Millions are dying slowly in our bloated prison system. Millions are dying while stuck in our ghettos, which are mostly death traps for poor and nonwhite people. Even our school systems play into this world of death, as they miseducate all citizens about the white American myths that run counter to what God is doing here and now. Right now justice is needed. Right now your own self-transformation is needed. Right now, your community can find deliverance by living into the birth, life, teachings, death, and resurrection of Jesus. We have lost sight of the reality that Jesus began a subversive and revolutionary movement in the midst of a troubled world.

Most people in the United States acknowledge that there is a racial problem, yet how we understand that problem varies greatly. It has become routine for Americans to watch videos of black bodies lying lifeless on the cement. With stifled imaginations socialized by the dominant view of what life ought to look like in society, we can't seem to get beyond our racialized conformity. We need the narrow way that leads us out. Therefore, a community that follows a pathway out of conformity to white supremacist patterns is needed, as it invites others to join in its experience of healing and deliverance.

My hope is that we as the church can rediscover our call to be that community. My hope is that we can visibly lead the way, groping together through the fog of racialized hierarchy and toward the light of Christ.

# EPILOGUE

As I conclude this book, another black person has been executed by police. Recently, during my last few weeks of editing, it seems that most of the black women and men being killed have died as a result of nothing more than "driving while black."

The reports of these killings remind me of an experience I had back when I was living in Harrisburg. I was pulled over by a cop, and as a young man in my early twenties at the time, I had a sense that I could die that night.

It was late. I didn't know why I had been pulled over, but eventually I found out that the registration sticker on the back of my car had expired; the month had changed a few days earlier. I had no clue that my car registration had lapsed.

The cop who pulled me over waited for a second police car to arrive. The second car parked across the road on a street that had a little traffic from time to time, but not a lot. The police officer driving the second car shone his bright headlights at my car. They were almost blinding, because it was dark and late at night. With the backup police car parked and ready, the first two police officers got out of their vehicle and approached my car.

My heart was already beating fast. I had no clue why I was being stopped, and I certainly couldn't fathom why a second car was needed. As the officers approached, I saw that one officer was coming up on the right side of the car and the other on the left. Both had already drawn their guns and had them pointed at me as they approached. They appeared ready to fire them if necessary.

I was terrified. Like always, I did what I had learned to do from the larger black community. No sudden movements. No reaching for anything in the car, whether in my pocket or the glove compartment, unless specifically asked. I had heard about unarmed black men who had been shot while reaching for their wallets or because the officer thought they had a gun or weapon.

No, that wasn't going to be me, so I kept my hands visible on the wheel. I moved awkwardly, in slow motion, and like a robot. That night, I spoke the most dominant-culture vernacular I could muster. I used my "suburban voice." I cowered before the police with a plethora of "Yes, sirs" and "No, sirs" and nods. After following all their requests, I received my ticket, they left, and I breathed a sigh of relief.

I have rarely told that experience to anyone, especially to white people. I have worried that listeners would think that such a story demonstrated that if you just "act right," everything will work out. The very real sense of fear that I felt and the possibility of actual death would be dismissed, I assumed, because I did not die that night. People might lose track of the fact that black youth are taught by their families, churches, and communities to dehumanize themselves in encounters with police just so they can stay alive. But if we are honest, following those strict guidelines still does not guarantee that we will make it home safely. We are taught not to break from the role of a submissive black man or woman in front of these gun-carrying officers sanctioned by the state.

That moment in which the officers approached me, guns drawn, wasn't about the lack of cultural exchange programs or pulpit swaps, or because black and white Christians hadn't sung enough warm, fuzzy songs of unity together every Sunday morning. It was about a racialized hierarchy expressed through a clear coercive power differential and a long history, centuries in the making. The policing system, no matter the racial makeup of its individual officers or how nice they are, is an extension and continuation of white supremacist powers that lord over many people's lives. That many white people's encounters with the police have left them feeling that such authorities are always there to serve and protect them, offering them a sense of security at night as they sleep in their homes—well, this frequently does not line up with my experiences with police, nor the encounters with police by my black friends, family, and neighbors.

Hearing these recent stories of black women and men driving their cars and dying in encounters with police—for mistaken identity, or a broken taillight, or not using a turn signal to change lanes—reminds me that my community and my Christian formation has prepared me to see society differently from how the dominant group frequently views it. Those of us who must navigate life on the underside of racial hierarchy require transformed minds and perceptions of society, because each of our lives depends on it.

Christians who live in the denial of such experiences don't know that their own transformation is intimately tied to coming alongside and learning from those at the bottom rung of our societal ladder. This is where Jesus has always chosen to be uniquely present. Jesus' delivering presence has always been especially available outside of the camp, where crucifixion takes place.

This is a portion of the trouble that I've seen. I hope I have passed it on to you as a gift, so that it might change how you view racism in America and ignite a new trajectory toward the way of Jesus. We must acknowledge that many of us have not just been sinners but, in this story of white supremacy, have first and foremost been sinned against. Grasping the gravity of the idolatrous violence and oppression that implicates us all, directly or indirectly, is not to cripple any of us in guilt or despair. Repentance opens up new possibilities available only through God revealed in Jesus Christ. Humbly, we can all come to the throne of grace in confidence, because we have a faithful High Priest who empathizes with our struggles. Here we can find help and deliverance in our time of need.

And certainly, as the church in America, we are in a time of need.

# ACKNOWLEDGMENTS

It wasn't a given that this book would be written when it was. It certainly was an awkward and untimely project in relation to my academic pursuits. And yet, considering the growing conversations and movements unfolding recently, the book felt like it was right on time.

Therefore, I must first acknowledge Amy Gingerich, who reached out to me and asked me to write a book for Herald Press that tackled the subject of racism and the church. I'm very grateful that she did. Next, I am compelled to repeatedly thank Valerie Weaver-Zercher for her careful editorial work at every step in the process, from conception to completion. She not only brought clarity and brevity to my words but also constructive feedback that immensely strengthened the content. Likewise, the entire Herald Press and MennoMedia team has been a pleasure to work with.

Other readers provided valuable input at key points in the project. Thank you, Hannah Heinzekehr, Tobin Miller Shearer, and Shavon Starling-Louis. A special thanks goes to Rodney Thomas, who provided a careful read of the text and who has been an important dialogue partner for me in a variety of ways.

Special thanks to Harrisburg Brethren in Christ Church and Montco Bible Fellowship. Though I couldn't possibly list every congregation, I must also thank the various Christian communities that have invited me into their gatherings to speak and dialogue with them on antiracism, racial justice, and the church. The majority of this book's concepts had a long process of maturation, having been refined primarily in talks, dialogues, and question and response sessions. I am also grateful for the people who took me seriously enough to ask the difficult questions that pushed me toward deeper reflection.

Thanks to the Department of Biblical and Religious Studies at Messiah College and the continued support I have received from many of my former professors. I am particularly grateful for Richard Crane's senior seminar, which was a timely course that gave me a thicker theological language to engage the problem of race and racism in society. And thank you to Reta Finger for teaching me the broader significance of Jesus' gospel. Similarly, I am indebted to Biblical Theological Seminary, particularly for the opportunity to pursue my master of divinity with an urban cohort of mostly black peers. Although I was the youngest one in the group, these friends and mentors always affirmed and recognized gifts in me that I hadn't fully seen in myself. It was a great faculty, of which Larry Anderson, Dan Williams, John Franke, Todd Mangum, and Derek Cooper deserve acknowledgment.

My educational journey also landed me at Lutheran Theological Seminary at Philadelphia. My doctoral cohort was filled with lively discussions, conviction-led disagreements, and intellectual debate that sharpened my own faith and theology. Gabe, Marva, and David, I value each of you, and look forward to seeing where your academic vocations lead you. Though this book is not my dissertation, it has certainly been strengthened by the clarifying questions that John Pahl, Nelson Rivera, and J. Denny Weaver bring to my work. But most importantly, Katie Day has been an amazing scholar to work under and with. From coursework, to my teaching assistant assignment, to conversations, to thinking about how she fluidly engages both the seminary and the broader community—all these things have been encouraging and influential.

Mom and Dad, I am completely indebted to the love I have received from you. Everything I do extends from that deep love. I have learned not to take it for granted.

Finally, to the person who is not only my life partner but one of the most significant dialogue partners and constructive critics while I try to make sense of the nonsense of our world, thank you, Renee. I love you and value your creativity, support, and perspective, all of which you bring to my life and all of which have direct influence on this book.

# THE AUTHOR

**D**rew G. I. Hart is a theologian, activist, blogger, and assistant professor at Messiah College. He received his PhD in theology and ethics from Lutheran Theological Seminary. His writing and speaking are informed by his ten years of pastoral ministry experience and his ongoing commitment to following Jesus. His blog, *Taking Jesus Seriously*, is hosted by *Christian Century*, and he speaks regularly at churches, universities, conferences, and seminaries. His writing has appeared in *Sojourners* and in books such as *Living Alternative: Anabaptist Christianity in a Post-Christendom World* and *Exploring the Gospel of Peace*. He also can be found on Twitter, @druhart, where he reflects on life and faith as it unfolds, and at www.drewgihart.com. He and his wife, Renee, have two young sons, Micah and Dietrich.